Twayne's English Authors Series

EDITOR OF THIS VOLUME

Kinley E. Roby

Northeastern University

William Sansom

TEAS 287

William Sansom

WILLIAM SANSOM

By LILA CHALPIN

Massachusetts College of Art

TWAYNE PUBLISHERS
A DIVISION OF G. K. HALL & CO., BOSTON

Frontispiece photo of William Sansom by Alan Clifton

Library of Congress Cataloging in Publication Data

Chalpin, Lila K
William Sansom.

(Twayne's English authors series; TEAS 287)
Bibliography: p. 150–52
Includes index.
1. Sansom, William, 1912–
—Criticism and interpretation.
PR6037.A75Z6   823'.9'14   79-21075
ISBN 0-8057-6781-9

For Kathryn and Marjorie

Contents

About the Author

Lila Chalpin is Associate Professor of Literature and Film at Massachusetts College of Art, where she has taught since 1970. She holds B.A. and M.A. degrees from the University of Wisconsin/Madison and the doctorate from Boston University. Professor Chalpin's principal areas of interest are modern British prose and poetry, and her essays, short stories, and poetry have appeared in *College English, English Journal, College Composition and Communication, College English Association Critic, Humanities Journal, Texas Quarterly, Ball State Forum, Kansas Quarterly, ERIC, Journal of General Education, Oyez!, Laurel Review* and *New Laurel Review*. She is co-editor of *Achievements in Fiction*.

Preface

William Sansom's name first came to my attention in 1950 when I was studying literature at the University of London. My tutor said he bore watching as one of the most promising new writers. In second-hand book shops I bought all the literary magazines I could find containing his short stories, *Fireman Flower, Something Terrible, Something Lovely,* and *The Body.* I also purchased books published by Sansom's contemporaries and a tea chest to pack them in. Upon disembarking in New York City, I heard from other passengers that the U.S. Customs was carefully inspecting all luggage for pornography. I felt confident that I would have no difficulty. But when it came my turn, the Customs Officer flung open my tea chest and grabbed a book, saying "*What* have we here?" The book in his hand was Sansom's *The Body.* Its cover was hot pink with an illustration of a fleshy woman draped in a hotter pink towel. I laughed and assured him thet *The Body* was not pornography but literature. And from that day to this, I have believed that *The Body* is literature and so is the majority of his works.

When William Sansom burst upon the postwar literary scene in Britain, English writers were sharply divided into experimentalists and realists, rebels and traditionalists, spokesmen for man's problems with the outside world and spokesmen for man's problems within himself. Experimentalists, such as Lawrence Durrell, William Golding, Iris Murdoch, Henry Green, and the so-called angry young men, John Wain and John Braine, tried new forms, as did James Joyce and Virginia Woolf earlier in the century. On the other hand, realistic writers, such as Pamela Hansford Johnson, Evelyn Waugh, Graham Greene, C. P. Snow, and Joyce Cary, eschewed the works of Joyce and Woolf and urged a return to the novel that told a story in the great tradition of the English novel. The furor caused by the partisans of experimental versus realistic writing was loud and vigorous.

Where did William Sansom stand in this furor? Curiously, he stood with both sides, depending on the form he used and when he wrote.

His early writing was short stories that were surrealistic. In the 1950s no avant-garde intellectual periodical in England was printed without either a Sansom short story or an announcement of a forthcoming one. His name became a touchstone for "new writing" and a "fresh point of view." Gradually, however, his writing became more traditional. By the 1960s, after he had proven his ability to write not only short stories but also essays and novels, critics began to judge where his forte was. Elizabeth Bowen called him "a short-storyist par excellence, a shortstoryist by birth, addiction and destiny." Frederick R. Karl observed that interest in class structure, the old staple of the English, had faded from most novels but not from Sansom's works. Sansom became known as the spokesman for the lower middle class English people. Some reviewers noted Sansom's emerging talent for comedy; still others found his use of landscape and objects masterly.

Critics often couple Sansom's name with Henry Green's and call them both minor novelists of the postwar decade. Although each is mainly known for his style and aesthetic views, they share no similarities. On the other hand, Sansom's short stories are sometimes anthologized with short stories by such contemporaries as Graham Greene, William Trevor, and Aldous Huxley.

Now, after thirty years of active writing and his recent death, Sansom's forty volumes of short stories, essays, and novels need to be appraised. Every critic seems to agree that his main interest was to write aesthetic prose. It is the aesthetic viewpoint rather than the moral, psychological, or societal that tempers his characterizations and plots. His two greatest strengths as a writer are his use of the senses in description that produces an immediate synaesthetic effect and his rendering of unusual points of view. While these strengths sometimes flower in his novels, they almost always flower in his short stories. Why the short story, which was his first love, is more compatible with his special gifts rather than the novel presents an interesting problem that this study will attempt to analyze. In doing so, I have given more plot summary and character description than would be needed in a book on a better-known writer. Although I have tried to be critical and analytical in my readings, I felt that my first obligation to both William Sansom's memory and the reader was to convey the sensation and essence of Sansom's works. This procedure also explains my liberal quoting of passages. This study begins with Sansom's life and early influences. Chapter 2 is an analysis of his early fiction, which for the most part was surrealistic and experimental.

Chapter 3 covers his nine novels with their weaknesses, strengths, and emerging comic touches. Chapters 4 through 6 delve into his unique creation of the travel–short story, the short story, and miscellaneous works that combine his early taste for the bizarre, later focus on romantic comedy, and final depiction of middle-aged, lower middle class English people. His talent for depicting these people seems to have made his works less accessible to readers in the United States, which accounts for why his work is not so well known here. I hope to prove why his work should be better known as creations of "something terrible, something lovely."

Several acknowledgments must be mentioned. I am deeply grateful to William Sansom, who allowed me to interview him on three occasions. I am indebted to the Berg Collection of the New York Public Library. I also wish to acknowledge the help and encouragement of many friends: Geoffrey Barraclough, Haskell M. Block, Elizabeth J. Buckley, Kathryn A. Coghlan, Marjorie Hellerstein, A. C. Hoffmann, and G. Alda Spencer.

LILA CHALPIN

Massachusetts College of Art
Boston, Massachusetts

Acknowledgments

I am indebted to the following for permission to reprint material in this book:

Elaine Greene, Ltd., for permission to quote from books by William Sansom:

Fireman Flower, Copyright © 1944; *Three*, Copyright © 1946; *The Body*, Copyright © 1949; *The Passionate North*, Copyright © 1950; *The Face of Innocence*, Copyright © 1951; *A Touch of the Sun*, Copyright © 1952; *Pleasures Strange and Simple*, Copyright © 1953; *A Bed of Roses*, Copyright © 1954; *The Loving Eye*, Copyright © 1956; *A Contest of Ladies*, Copyright © 1956; *Among the Dahlias*, Copyright © 1957; "Coming to London," *Coming to London*, Copyright © 1957; *The Cautious Heart*, Copyright © 1958; *Blue Skies, Brown Studies*, Copyright © 1960; *The Last Hours of Sandra Lee*, Copyright © 1961; *The Stories of William Sansom*, Copyright © 1963; *The Ulcerated Milkman*, Copyright © 1966; *Goodbye*, Copyright © 1966; *Hans Feet in Love*, Copyright © 1971; *The Birth of a Story*, Copyright © 1972; *A Young Wife's Tale*, Copyright © 1974.

Hodder and Stoughton, Ltd., and Society of Authors for permission to quote from *South* by William Sansom.

Little Brown and Company for permission to quote from *Collected Stories of William Sansom*, and *The Last Hours of Sandra Lee*.

Russell and Volkening, Inc., for permission to quote from the *The Face of Innocence*, *The Body*, and *A Bed of Roses*.

Chronology

1912 William Sansom born in London, son of Ernest Brooks, a banker, and Mabel Clark.

1920- Attended Uppingham School
1928

1928- Studied German in Bonn. Traveled extensively in Europe to
1930 learn languages for banking business.

1930 Trained in Anglo-German Bank in London.

1935 Worked as a copyeditor in an advertising agency where he met Norman Cameron and his circle of writer-friends. Composed jazz and had a waltz accepted by the Folies Bergère in Paris. Worked as a dance-pianist and helped to run a nightclub.

1939 Joined the National Fire Service for the duration of World War II.

1941- Published first stories in *Horizon, Cornhill, New Writing and*
1944 *Daylight, Penguin New Writing,* and *Writing Today.*

1944 *Fireman Flower.*

1945- *Three.* Worked as script writer for a film company. Received
1946 award from Society of Authors.

1947 *Westminster at War.* Received award from Society of Authors and quit film company for full-time literary life. Began travel assignments for *Lilliput, World Review, Geographical Magazine,* and other travel magazines. For the next twenty-five years, wrote countless essays and travel–short stories which were periodically collected in volumes.

1948 *Equilibriad, Something Terrible, Something Lovely,* and *South.*

1949 *The Body.*

1950 *The Passionate North.*

1951 *The Face of Innocence.* Elected a Fellow of the Royal Society of Literature.

1952 *A Touch of the Sun.*

1953 *It Was Really Charlie's Castle, The Light That Went Out,* and *Pleasures Strange and Simple.*

1954   Married Ruth Grundy, an actress and mother of two sons, Sean and Nicholas, by a former marriage. *Lord Love Us* and *A Bed of Roses.*

1956   *The Loving Eye* and *A Contest of Ladies.*

1957   *Among the Dahlias.*

1958   *The Cautious Heart* and *The Icicle and the Sun.*

1960   *Blue Skies, Brown Studies.*

1961   *The Last Hours of Sandra Lee.*

1963   *The Stories of William Sansom, Get-Well Quick Colouring Book* (ed. and illus.) and *Who's Zoo,* ed. Michael Brande (illus.).

1964   *Away to It All.*

1966   *The Ulcerated Milkman* and *Goodbye.*

1968   *The Grand Tour* and *Christmas.*

1969   *The Vertical Ladder.*

1971   *Hans Feet in Love.*

1972   *The Birth of a Story.*

1973   *The Marmalade Bird* and *Proust and His World.*

1974   *A Young Wife's Tale, Victorian Life in Photographs,* and *Skimpy.*

1976   Died in London on April 20.

CHAPTER 1

The Making of a Writer

WILLIAM Sansom burst into print in London, in 1944, with a Kafkaesque collection of short stories entitled *Fireman Flower*. These short stories are fictional accounts of his experiences as a fireman during the fire-bombings that devastated much of London. After the appearance of this collection, he extended his storytelling talents to novellas, novels, children's stories, essays, and travel pieces.

When demobilization came, he did not return to his prewar job with an advertising agency. Instead, he worked as a script writer for a film company. But, as his stories gained acceptance in fine literary magazines such as *Horizon, Penguin New Writing, Orpheus,* and *New Writing and Daylight,* he soon decided to quit the film company and risk the purely literary life. The result of this decision was a series of prizes, honors, and a traveling scholarship in the late 1940s and 1950s and success until his death in 1976.

The outstanding characteristic of his work is his vivid, sensuous description. Whether he is describing the white-collar class of Londoners who were his neighbors or exotic landscapes for his unique travel stories, he always is able to indulge in what he has called his favorite form of receation—"watching."

In a hand-written notebook entitled "The Impossibility of Being Billy," Sansom has written of his childhood. An only child, born to comfortable middle-class parents, Sansom was raised in London, attended school at Uppingham, and was thought to be destined for a career in commercial banking.

His early memories of himself as Billy are sketched humorously. He claims to have spent his infant hours in a pram peering upwards, cogitating the sounds of the universe. At two, he fell in love with a parking meter, which may help explain his writing talent for lovingly describing inanimate objects. At eight, he fell in love with a dark-haired girl named Lila Hooper. To the melody of the song "Swanee," he used to sing: "Lila/ how I love you/ how I love you" for hours. As a child he wrote stories and verse and practiced the piano faithfully. During adolescence he was more interested in song-writing than writing. But, socially at parties and at dancing class, he remained shy and awkward. As he matured, his self-consciousness increased; he feared he had a poor physique and ugly buck teeth. Even as an adult, disguised by a beard and embonpoint, he confessed to still feeling awkward about his body.[1]

In another hand-written notebook, "A Map of My Skin," he recounts memories from eight to ten years of age. These memories mark what became his greatest talent: the ability to recreate not visual imagery so much as the more difficult imagery of sound, touch, and smell. His father, a naval architect, provided a comfortable home for his family and filled it with his own painted copies of artwork from the Tate Gallery. Sansom recalls the sound of horses, wheels, his mother speaking on the phone, the gritty turn of an old knife-sharpening machine in the kitchen, the lively pitch of tradesmen's voices, and the smell of paint on his balcony and of old copper.

His bedroom overlooked a tennis club. By day he would hear the put-put of tennis balls and see men wielding tennis racquets, dressed in white flannel trousers. By night he could feel the "dull, aching air" and envy the tennis players who were still awake and playing when children had to go to bed. Later he would hear sounds of music and merriment. In his pajamas he would creep out on the balcony and look down through the balustrade with envy. Being an only child, he was with grownups often; thus, the memories of the long, lonely hours in his room were sharp.

At nine he caught scarlet fever and lived in isolation in his room for six weeks. Only his mother was allowed into the room to care for him. His immediate joy was not having to attend school. But the isolation of not being allowed beyond the balcony rails was annoying. Since his father went to work daily, he was not allowed to visit the sick room. But Sansom smelled his father through the turpentine he used as he painted art copies on Sunday and Sansom saw him from afar dashing across the tennis courts in his white flannels.

His most vivid memory was of skin peeling off his kneecap whole. It was pure parchment and he thought of it as a pirate map. It was a great loss when it had to be destroyed because it was thought to be infectious.

He writes of this period as one "not only of fever isolation but also mental isolation . . . an advanced course in egocentricity. . . . I suppose I became . . . a snail—great eyes peering out on stalks [from the balcony] but ramming back into my shell at any sign of interference. I have remained a snail ever since."[2]

When he finished preparatory school he chose to study German in Bonn in preparation for a career in banking which his father had long ago set as a desirable goal. In 1930 he returned to London and worked at an Anglo-German bank for five years. Living in his parents' comfortable home with its established order and training at a bank with its established order did not succeed in lulling his artistic senses. He wrote songs, lyrics, and sketches for cabarets. One of these songs, a waltz, was accepted by the Folies Bergère of Paris.

Finally, in 1935 at the age of twenty-three, he left home and banking to become a copywriter at an advertising agency. He continued writing jazz and at night often worked as a pianist and helped run a nightclub. He later drew upon this experience in writing his novel *The Cautious Heart*. But more important than either his work or his music was the sharing of an office at the advertising agency with the man who was to have the greatest influence on his work—Norman Cameron. Cameron was a poet and translator of Villon, Rimbaud, Voltaire, and Balzac. Robert Graves in the introduction to *The Collected Poems of Norman Cameron* says, ". . . He was a divided character—alternately a Presbyterian precisian and moralist, and a pagan poet and boon-companion."[3]

Cameron was a ruthless self-critic; hence his small output of poems. He destroyed much more of what he wrote than he preserved. But, as James Reeves notes, in a commemorative issue of the *Review*,

No poet, however indifferent he may appear to fame, is indifferent about the impact he makes. Norman's poems were not "successful" in any obvious sense. . . . He was what is called a poets' poet: no poet of any standing was unaware of him, but he made no general impact, was never fashionable, never intruded on the empire achieved in the thirties and forties by others less good, in my opinion, and more modish than he.[4]

Sansom described Cameron as a strange, tall man with a mass of uncombed hair, who always carried a lot of poetry books to the office. He enjoyed copywriting and brought to it, in the words of Graves, "the same passionate exactitude that he applied to his poems. It amused him to find out all he could about the manufacture of ice cream, cheese-spreads, tonic wines, or whatever . . . and then set his precise imagination to the task of selling them."[5]

What Sansom learned from Cameron about the use of precise words and the beauty of Rimbaud's poetry was continued after work in a local wine-shop. There he met several of Norman's friends:

... an astounded cherub called Thomas, a clerkly-looking fellow called Gascoyne, egg-domed Len Lye like an ascetic coster in his raffish cap, and many more.... Unlike certain other writers *manqués* back in the office, they did not discuss literary theory or whine about their souls and sensitivities—they made up things there and then, grabbed down extraordinary stories and myths from the air, wrote down doggerel and verse.[6]

Besides stimulating Sansom to write, Cameron and his friends, who were all radicals and sympathized with the Loyalists in the Spanish Civil War, made him feel disloyal to his father. His father was at that time building ships for the Spanish navy. Sansom felt guilty over his unpolitical attachments to the wrong side while his new friends were seething to get at the fascists. He said, "I felt wrong and yet right; but always out on the other side of an extraordinary fence made of bowler-hats and Omar Khayyam, saxophones, and golf bags."[7]

Cameron also was the catalyst in a moment of epiphany for Sansom. When Cameron took him to the surrealist exhibition on Burlington Street, Sansom immediately understood what all the other paintings he had seen until that moment lacked. "Here were these surrealists . . . at last blowing the old, old story sky-high! I was immediately addicted forever. I was under no delusion that they painted the subconscious: *theirs was a plain statement of reality.*"[8] Almost any novel or short story that he was to write after this epiphany revealed exactly how addicted he became to personal interpretations of reality.

After this important discovery, war broke out and another important person became his friend—Fernando Henriques, a scholar of West-Indian extraction. Sansom met Henriques when he joined the Fire Brigade at Kensington and was posted at Hampstead. Sansom and Henriques discussed modern and classical literature as Sansom never did before or since in his life. He gradually found his old dream of making a future career in the world of entertainment fading and began to start seriously to write stories.[9]

Soon his experiences in the Fire Brigade became the subject of his writing. They were collected in *Fireman Flower*, which created critical acclaim when it was published in 1944. Those stories depicted the nightmarish reality of moments during the war. They were called Kafkaesque, and they will be discussed at length in Chapter 2.

After the war he worked for a short time as a script writer for a film company. But as his stories gained more recognition he decided to leave the film company and risk everything on his ability to write. From that time until his death he wrote full time. In between novels and short stories he wrote travel assignments in a unique form: he would set short stories in particular exotic places. These travel–short stories are among his best works. He also worked on essays about art, people, and emotions for various magazines in Britain and the United States.

For many years he lived as a bachelor. His fiction gradually changed from the early allegorical themes to romantic and comic themes. In 1954 he married Ruth Grundy, an actress and literary agent. With her two sons by a former marriage they moved to St. John's Wood. These sons undoubtedly inspired him to write children's books also.

He moved his family to a home in St. John's Wood, where he lived until his death in 1976. He attributed St. John's Wood with having had a salutary effect on his writing. In particular, he found his street, Hamilton Terrace, the closest thing in London to a boulevard, slow and tranquilizing.

The slowness [of the Wood] is a wonder. Without going near a main road, we have three separate shopping villages, all with shopkeepers whom we know personally. You cannot buy a simple tin of baked beans without discussing arthritis, ulcers or the gallantry of the sub-postmistress who has been severely raided. And there is constant talk of the weather—for a Londoner here is just as weatherwise as a countryman, everyone knows where the wind is, how rain-bearing are the clouds. We smell the coming of snow as a West End PRO smells the arrival of a steak Diane.[10]

Thus one can understand how this ambience helped Sansom write of ordinary things in a fresh style. The longer he lived there, the more his characters appeared to be drawn upon his neighbors. He enjoyed daily shopping trips and visits to the local pub until the end of his life when he had difficulty walking. He would stop and chat with his favorite tradesmen and would unconsciously absorb their locutions and mannerisms. Here is his description of them:

The local independent plumber has no office nor telephone nor staff for you to pay for: his office is a free and permanently unchanged three feet at the bar of The Drum and Monkey, where pipes may always be discussed between 13 and 15 hours. There is [also] one of the last art-greengrocers in London. As fishmongers used to make brilliant abstract fish-pictures of their slabs, so does this greengrocer with his window. Perfect pyramids of oranges, apples triangled like a snare of snooker balls, red cabbages balanced perfectly against green, a palm-like pineapple naughtily nested among an eggy brood of sprouts even a parsnip given some kind of temporary beauty. All this is built up with loving care every day and in a most unpretentious back-street. The same short street, in fact, whose other end houses another greengrocer called Dance, through whose lighted window I once saw what must have been Mr. Dance waltzing with a lady whom I trust was Mrs. Dance among the potatoes and carrots of their trade.

And there is Mr. France, who painted the numbers on most of the doors and gateposts in our part of The Wood. . . . He had been a merchant seaman turned cinema organist. Somewhere or other Mr. France and his Wurlitzer rose from the ex-orchestra pit and gave forth live music like *The Rustle of Spring* at intervals when nowadays the audience is conned into buying ice-cream.[11]

These tradesmen of the lower middle class gave a sense of "local color" to almost all of Sansom's novels and many short stories. In fact, he became a spokesman for the London middle class along with just a handful of his contemporaries. Frederick R. Karl says,

Class has assumed a large importance only in a number of the humorists, Waugh, Powell . . . L. P. Hartley, Olivia Manning, V. S. Pritchett, Angus Wilson, and William Sansom. However, these writers either use class differences strictly for comic purposes . . . or else lack at least at this stage of their development the artistic intensity to make class conflicts meaningful.[12]

This study will demonstrate that Sansom used class differences not for political purposes but strictly for comic purposes.

Writing full time demanded some sacrifices and compromises. In the late 1940s he received grants and traveling scholarships. Later on he was commissioned by *Holiday* magazine to write essays on Denmark, Sweden, and Finland. This commission resulted in a commercial form of prose-writing that took precedence over writing novels or short stories because the pay was lucrative. In fact, he said a couple of travel articles paid him as much as the royalties earned from a novel.[13] In addition, the market for short stories shrank during the 1960s and 1970s so that he felt forced to compromise with the times by writing more essays for commercial magazines. Yet, he continued to write novels, most of which were not successful. Some critics suggest he did this because the novel sold better than the short story which is the genre that suits his talent best. Obviously his investment of time and energy in the novel rather than in the short story was determined by many factors: the more lucrative rewards of novels; the challenge to master a form that did not come to him easily; and the wish to improve on his craft after each novel was thoroughly analyzed by the critics.

Having never had a private income, he learned to live cautiously, saving a certain amount of money no matter how low his income. Even with prosperity he enjoyed trips to second-hand clothing stores to buy dead men's suits at bargain prices. He also followed the advice of his neighbors in the pub who helped him avoid expensive repairs on his home by teaching him how to mend things by himself.[14]

The ambivalence he felt toward writing for entertainment (and income) and writing for literary achievement continued throughout his last twenty years of life. Nevertheless, he has always tried to turn reality into something terrible or something lovely. His interests are neither political, social, nor psychological, but aesthetic. In an interview he criticized contemporary authors for

> . . . sneering at life, breaking it down, without building it up, writing about, for instance, continually washing up in the kitchen, with the grey daylight coming through now and again, strikes the bar of soap and illuminates the whole dreary kitchen with an absolutely glorious feeling.[15]

While this statement applies more to the angry young men of the 1950s and the "kitchen sink" school, it reveals much about Sansom's reading habits, too. He was evidently reading works by his contemporaries who were commanding headlines rather than works by those contemporaries who were steadily producing quality fiction such as C. P. Snow, Angus Wilson, Lawrence Durrell, Joyce Cary, and Iris Murdoch. The latter group of writers produced works still read and talked about today, but the same cannot be said for the writers of the "kitchen sink school." Even fifteen years after this denunciation by Sansom he preferred not to read his contemporaries but to reread the works of four writers, Poe, Proust, Bunin, and Rhys. While the influence of these four writers may at times seem subtle, it shall be demonstrated in various works of Sansom.

CHAPTER 2

Early Fiction: Kafkaesque Nightmares and Obsessions

S ANSOM'S early stories, consisting of three collections, *Fireman Flower* (1944), *Three* (1946), *The Equilibriad* and *Something Terrible, Something Lovely* (1948), dwell mainly on the experiences of firemen during the Second World War, allegories of man's search for harmony in life, and peak emotional experiences. Most of the endings reveal man's inability to change the "terrible" elements of life into "lovely" elements.

I   Fireman Flower

In his first published collection of fireman stories, Sansom reveals himself, according to the critics, as being under the influence of Franz Kafka. His characters carefully weigh and measure illusions against a background of reality. Their stream-of-consciousness monologues resemble a philosopher's search for reason.

Wittgenstein says, "Philosophy simply puts everything before us, and neither explains nor deduces anything. . . . The work of the philosopher consists in assembling reminders for a particular purpose."[1] Sansom, as a philosopher-fiction writer, does just this in his early fiction. He writes of ordinary London working-class people confronting philosophical puzzles as common happenings. They quest after illusions as a solution to reality but finally recognize that survival without one or the other is impossible. Man needs both illusion and reality.

The longest story of *Fireman Flower* is the story "Fireman Flower." It draws upon Sansom's experiences as a fireman. Fireman Flower, a volunteer with the Fire Brigade, searches a warehouse for the source of a fire caused by a German bomb. John Vickery sees this search as "an allegorical account of a metaphysical quest that ends, somewhat like Hesse's *Journey to the East*, with the recognition that the quest was illusory but necessary."[2]

As Fireman Flower, the leader of his crew, seeks the kernel of the fire along corridors and endless staircases, his two companions serve as foils. Like an epic hero on a quest, Flower is engulfed by self-doubts, distrust of his companions, and delusions. When his two companions disagree about which door of the warehouse to enter, Flower pauses in doubt.

True, he had forgotten about his companions. But that had been due only to the eagerness of his arrival. He knew quite well that he would have remembered them soon enough. This behavior of theirs was most odd—he had never seen his companions disagree before. And surely they would hardly presume to question his own orders?[3]

When they finally do follow him up the steps, he feels irritated that they have sown a "germ of doubt" in his mind. This irritation is the major emotion that Sansom depicts. Flower's self-doubts instigate a battle of his will between action and inaction. His intellect also seems to perceive truth but then realizes it is perceiving a distortion of truth.

In the midst of a real struggle with the kernel of the fire, Flower experiences, within the passing smokey air, a range of emotions analogous to a life experience.

Sometimes the smoke cleared to reveal some object of the surrounding chaos, only to reclose around it almost before it could be properly registered by the eye and the mind; so that the object held no permanence, so that it seemed to have been only a flutter of the imagination, a half-remembered episode from the dreamed past.[4]

He realizes he has almost succumbed to the vision of an imaginary fire. As he notices his companions' uncertainty, he begins to feel more comfortable with his own uncertainty. He admits to himself that he may be too easily led. "Or is the appearance of things at first so persuasive that it deceives each man? Still . . . I must be careful. Now I know I must reject more perhaps than I wish."[5] He realizes that getting rid of his doubts is not security in itself, not pure freedom. It is merely freedom from doubt, the greatest deception of all. Thus Fireman Flower realizes that the problem has not been made simpler. Rather it has been clarified as possessing a multiplicity of aspects.

As in Kafka's stories, Fireman Flower goes through a series of dreamlike surrealistic experiences fraught with the unknown, dread, and guilt over undifferentiated experiences in his past life. Small events assume the same importance as big events. Every encounter with an aspect of the fire is a trial of life and death until he begins to tolerate his own illusions. The ravaging fire suggests an allegory of the forces of life. In a London store, the stairs and corridors are comparable to highways in life. The kernel of the fire suggests the purpose of life that all men seek. Some allegorical effects are achieved in the perfume department, where the fumes of cosmetics and powders compare to the shallow materialism of British life; the immensity of the store and the cosmic heat of the fire compare to a warning of the apocalypse; and the quiet homelife of his escapist friend which Flower remembers in the middle of fire-fighting compares to worldly norms and laws.

Flower's triumph comes when he and his companions finally find the seat of the fire. As water pours out of the hoses and sparks jet around them, Flower thinks, "At last I have come face to face with the essence of things! Here is the abstract! Here is a brave new romance! Here is the violent, quintessential magma for which the spirit has thirsted! Here is reason!"[6] As he breaks through the roof, both literally and figuratively, he feels aware of life's mysteries with love and acceptance. Thus man accepts his own essence as a cipher in an alienated world. In an existential sense, he must make every moment in this life meaningful. If he does not, the world will continue to hold for him smoke, smog, and an absence of self-clarity.

Sansom's ability to anthropomorphize certain objects—a storage tank full of gasoline, a boiler on the point of bursting—supplies motivation for what little human action his characters take. Ronald Mason says,

. . . It is the precise and logical projection by an unusually vivid imagination of an instinctive feeling that in the machine and its unpredictable destructive power man has met his match. The physical dwarfing of Sansom's humans in face of their terrifying and masterful machines is an exact representation of the spiritual dwarfing of mankind in face of the overpowering onset of scientific and industrial progress. It is not an original thought, of course, and it is not even a particularly profound one, but it happens to be felt on their pulses by many artists and writers; and the way that Sansom has chosen to express in imaginative form what he has felt intuitively is original enough to make his development of it of real and suggestive value. The mystery and horror of the result is a perfectly genuine reflection of the mystery and horror of many aspects of the present stage of civilization.[7]

In another story, "In the Maze," Sansom draws an allegory based on mechanized life. The Topiarist, eternally clipping the hedges of a gigantic maze, explains to a tourist about the colony of people who live within the hedges. Like the citizens of *Brave New World*, no one in the maze ages. People spend their days clipping the yew trees that comprise the maze. This natural vegetation contrasts with the perfect engineering of a nearby city. The maze has no entrance or exit. People must cut their way into it. Life within is run according to the grand design of the founder, the Arboretor. He had led the people away from the city into the maze so that they could "exercise purely in the squares they love, but at the same time they are able to see what they do."[8] Confinement in a square of the maze would keep the brain from overworking and allow it to "stand aside from itself and survey its work."[9] The maze suggests heaven. It is a place where there is a sense of stability and harmony; it is removed from the chaos of the present. But it substitutes boredom for creativity, repetition for deep emotions.

In contrast with this attainable heaven, "The Forbidden Lighthouse" describes an Eden which man may never reenter. Like many of the stories by Joseph Conrad, "The Forbidden Lighthouse" implies a moral about man's penance for alienating himself first from the land and then from the lighthouse. Erland Lagerroth says of the lighthouse:

It rises on a rock in a sea which is boundless, changeable and evasive like wishes and dreams, and by its height, its light and also, of course, its distance, it arouses a sentimental admiration in the population. . . . But restraint in some harbour captain has made the population withdraw from everything which concerns the lighthouse, and this is a way of describing the puritanical spirit.[10]

Terence and Moon, the young couple who finally make their way through authorities and a rocky coast to the lighthouse, are freedom-seeking people. But, when they finally achieve their end, the lighthouse becomes the death of a dream. The couple then search for a new dream after alienating themselves first from the shore and then from the lighthouse. They are condemned to be in exile as each dream turns into a reality that has lost its allure.

"The Peach-House Potting Shed" is reminiscent of Kafka's *The Castle*. An old gardener who lives in the peach-house potting shed must survive a long apprenticeship before the Estate Office will grant him his appointment. Every now and then officers of the Estate Office break the gardener's solitude by providing him with the latest literature and information. He cultivates the fruit actively and then muses upon his cultivations.

Nevertheless he suffers attacks of restiveness. One such attack drives him out of the hot-house and into the wood to contemplate the busy, cooperative life of an ant colony. Then he becomes guilty that he has interrupted his contemplations to watch the ants for an hour.

When he returns to the hot-house, the hose, abandoned on the floor, has flooded the place. This seems just punishment to him, rendered by unseen forces.

Then a gentleman arrives to occupy the garden. The Estate Office warns the gardener not to disturb the gentleman, but eventually both men become attracted to each other and strive to meet. Again unseen forces intervene to prohibit their breaking the rules of the Estate Office. The gardener becomes entangled in the branches of one of his peach trees and the gentleman, in running toward the door of the hot-house, becomes entangled in his cloak.

The next day, the villagers have to scale the wall to drag the half-dead men to safety. There they tenderly embrace one another. And the story ends with these words: "Yes, it was only through the agency of others that the need for others was fulfilled in that embrace. Only through the agency of us, the others."[11] Sansom's moral may be interpreted in two ways: either man must find out the correct channels to establish relationships, which suggests an ironic view of a conformist society, or man must pay with his life in order to enlist the aid of "others," the unseen forces, to gain a few moments of fulfillment, which suggests a mystical view of man's place in the universe.

Critics have disagreed about Sansom's debt to Kafka in this story. Peter F. Neumeyer says,

The arbitrary, omniscient, impersonal, and all powerful Estate Office is so obviously of the same city as the Gate of the Law and as the Castle, and the gardener and the gentleman, so close and yet never communicating, are so clearly of the desperate family of Joseph K. and Gregor Samsa, that the author can hardly be thought to have wanted to conceal his debt. These similarities are, however, not "externals"; they are mirrorings of a view of man's essential isolation.[12]

Neumeyer believes these similarities are not casual but represent a view Sansom shares with Kafka of a deterministic universe.

In contrast with Neumeyer, Paulette Michel-Michot feels that he ignores the significance of the peach-house and potting-shed. She says, "Sansom presents 'situations' which he deliberately builds in order to teach something. . . . The teacher comes out in the last paragraph." There, she feels, Sansom points to man's fundamental need for others through joy and suffering. Like the ant episode earlier in the story in which the gardener yearns for a life within a community, the last paragraph is a fruition of that yearning.[13] Kafka's concluding paragraphs have never contained such yearnings or fruition of these yearnings.

Sansom himself in an interview claimed not to have read Kafka at the time that he wrote these stories. He did, however, admit to a belief in unseen forces that haunt houses, such as his own, and people.[14] Certainly the gardener's yearning for others is not Kafkaesque. Kafka's characters yearn for freedom from fear and guilt and acceptance by a higher authority. But they do not yearn for love and companionship. Sansom appears to be offering his own ideas about alienation and the solution to it.

Perhaps the story most influenced by science fiction in *Fireman Flower* is "The Long Sheet." Groups of captives are held in cubicles through which a long sheet, heavy with water, passes. The warders tell the captives that when the task of wringing the sheet dry is completed, they will be granted their freedom. Since the sheet hangs low and the cubicles are full of steam, the task will take months.

Different captives react differently to the task. In one room, all five worked earnestly. They wanted their freedom. In another room, some captives avoid the reality of the sheet and will never be free. Others seek shortcuts by bribery. In another room, the captives do not feel the vision of a better future is an incentive to work. They succeed in making the sheet wetter instead of drier. In yet another room, the captives are successful. They feel that

it is not the production that counts, but the life lived in the spirit during production. Production, the tightening of the muscles, the weaving of the hands, the pouring forth of shaped materials—this is only an employment for the nervous body, the dying legacy of the hunter's will to movement. Let the hands weave, but at the same time let the spirit search. Give the long sheet its rightful place—and concentrate on a better understanding of the freedom that is our real object.[15]

These captives achieve their ends because they have faith. They realize that freedom lies in an attitude of the spirit which they already have. Freedom is defined in this story not as a state of physical movement outside of prison but as a state of mind. This theme is didactically stated at the end.

After reading the stories in *Fireman Flower*, Peter Nevile predicted that Sansom might depart from allegorical influences and "turn to a more realistic and less obscure story."[16] His prediction came true, but not in the form of realism as it was known in the 1940s.

II   Three

Two years after *Fireman Flower, Three* was published. *Three* consists of two short stories, "Cat Up a Tree" and "The Invited," and a novella, "The Cleaner's Story." It is only in the latter that Sansom reveals new form.

"The Cleaner's Story" is a tour de force. The entire point of view is rendered by a cleaner who, on her hands and knees scrubbing the floor of a French café from 11:00 A.M. to 1:00 P.M., tells the story. The idea for this point of view occurred to Sansom when he saw René Clair's film *Le Million*. It is about factory life filmed from a completely different angle. *Le Million* fused with Sansom's own experience of scrubbing floors in the Fire Brigade and sitting, as a child, under a table, half-hearing the conversation of grown-ups.[17]

The cleaner, a woman of gentle birth whose family has lost its money, overhears the conversation of the diners while cleaning the floor at their feet. She is intelligent. Her solace for the degrading turn of events in her life that has made her a worker is her sense of urgency in her job. She seeks temporary order—a clean floor for luncheon. And she amuses herself with observations about the petty greed and jealousy of diners seated above her. Here are some of her observations:

. . . Some of them pretend not to notice me. But they are wrong! I am not in the least embarrassed. Although I am on my knees, which of course they think is humiliating, I am not in the least humiliated. In fact it is I who scorn them. I feel that I'm getting on with something. My muscles are working while they chatter, while they pose, disarranging their lives, striving perpetually to get things straight, yet merely disarranging matters more; while I, I am the person who is constantly straightening things out, keeping life fit to live in.[18]

Her unique point of view also makes her aware of how deceptive things are. Everything she hears becomes significant because it is half-heard. She realizes that her impressions change from minute to minute, thus illustrating the interplay between illusion and reality.

Sansom is intuitively aware of what psychologists call "'foot-speak' . . . one of the most expressive . . . of all our 'inner voices' not only through the habitual posture and movements of the foot, but in the way we dress the foot with shoes. . . . It is expressive in revealing our psychosexual attitudes along with participating directly in . . . sexual arousal."[19] From looking at a pair of shoes, the cleaner comes to some interesting conclusions revealing idiosyncrasies and social conflict.

The yellowish canvas shoes of M. Fandouk, the much-travelled M. Fandouk who once owned ten servants and now cherishes canvas shoes—these shoes that knew the glories of the Tunisian sun sit with their heels together and their toes turned out. They sit like the haunches of a dog with worms. They splay out, seeking comfort, with a lot of question in them. If they started to walk, the body above them would sway from side to side with a sing-song motion. They are quite certain of themselves, and yet full of interest, full of question. That's why they point outwards, like noses sniffing at either direction.[20]

Sansom's personification of shoes as a dog with worms is undoubtedly influenced by his admiration of the lithography of Grandville. Grandville depicted animal-headed humans acting out human comedies. The effect of his images is weird and surrealistic. In an essay on Grandville which he later expanded as a preface to a book on the artist that was never published, Sansom says,

Evidence of the phantom, of the demon, of a fixed staring truth that, if it does not horrify, disquiets us with its statement of facts not humanly understandable, extra-historic, only-to-be-whispered-of, and never to be judged by our own, incomplete knowledge of the world.[21]

In another passage, Sansom creates through the cleaner's senses not only anthropomorphized shoes but anthropomorphized feet and legs. The effect is disquieting.

Let Mme. Tissot stride in on her high black heels. . . . let old Michel smoke his pipe among the white chairs. . . . Let Nanon de Tous burst into her leathery old laugh and bustle up the old echoes with her pirate feet. Let them all come. Perhaps they are right. Perhaps it's time they took possession. Fat bursting legs, thin wanting legs, yellow tropical shoes, shining pointed lawyer's shoes, shining black heels, modest grey stockings, dull-black, workaday boots, gaunt Rose Meyer's wool slippers, Nanon's buttoned boots—let them all come mincing and bustling and clattering over the old mosaic and make what they want of it.[22]

What the cleaner makes of it is an amusing tale of human folly. The story ends at 1:00 P.M. with the end of lunch. The cleaner is once again left alone in the café, accepting the cleaning process as a rhythm of decay and renewal like a character from the stories of *Fireman Flower*. But, unlike the characters in that volume, the cleaner has a sense of humor. This adds a new dimension to Sansom's craft which grows with his art.

III   The Equilibriad

Another novella, *The Equilibriad*, appeared in a limited edition in 1948, two years after *Three* but closely related to "The Cleaner's Story" in its use of an unusual point of view. The point of view in *The Equilibriad* is of a man whose sense of balance has been disrupted.

Paul, a bachelor of forty, awakens to find he is skidding uncontrollably. He reduces the duties of his day to walking to his office, collecting his mail, and meeting the train on which his mistress-cousin Ada will arrive that afternoon. In the course of trying to get dressed, his knees suddenly buckle and then become taut again; he nearly loses his balance when moving but regains it when close to the danger of falling; he feels drunk, but realizes he is tilted at a slant. He cannot figure out rationally why his balance is awry. But as he ventures out on the street and bystanders laugh at his erratic walk, he suddenly finds he is enjoying himself.

Here were all the sensations of danger, wedded to the knowledge that the danger would finally, at the last hair-breadth moment, be averted. He felt himself veering over, felt the palms of his hands sweat to clutch out and save himself, felt his heart beat, the breath catch in his throat, his face flinch and his spirit gulp—as though the whole fleshed organism inside him were rising to combat his unbalance. And then, instantly, even during these sensations, the knowledge that he would never fall calmed him, so that somehow he experienced a mounting and a subsidence of emotion at exactly the same time.[23]

Here Sansom controls the grotesque so masterfully that the reader as well as the victim is amused yet discomforted.

Paul is diverted by his new malady and does not think of anything else. He does not notice that his office clerks are grave and obsequious when he skitters around them. He momentarily questions their obsequy but concludes that most clerks possess it. He feels at a loss to explain his unbalance because he does not yet understand it.

When his mistress-cousin, Ada, alights from the train, she does not notice his awkwardness. Only in the restaurant does she, quite out of character, command him to stop looking drunk. As she barks at him, her usual "oblong calf-face" with its slavish features changes to that of a virago. Paul is surprised to find her company is actually pleasing to him for a change.

But his new-found pleasure in Ada is doomed because she has come to punish him for making her into a "kept" woman. She announces that she has met another man, who is awaiting them.

On a ruse she leads Paul to the empty waiting room of the train station. She grabs a long bamboo cane she finds there and menaces Paul with it. While she vents her anger on him, he tries to tell her about his new-found understanding of himself and need of her.

The grab-hook came down through the air at him. Perhaps Ada had been infuriated by his words. . . . Paul had no time to enquire, he was too concerned with his own thought. His only desire was to express to another the truth revealed to him. The revelation had overwhelmed him. Already it was forming itself into a conception greater than before, immeasurably embracing. He had suddenly ceased to regard his obsession clinically as an exterior phenomenon. Now he realised that he too was part of the pattern. He saw that he must . . . adapt himself to new ways.[24]

The use of the word *obsession* in this passage bears implications not only for Paul's immediate reactions but for most of the future protagonists of Sansom's novels. It foreshadows the obsessional jealousy of Henry, of *The Body*, the obsessional lying of Eve, of the *Face of Innocence*, the obsessional voyeurism of Ligne, of *The Loving Eye*, and the obsessional possessiveness of the narrator of *The Cautious Heart*.

Paul uses his new insight to his own advantage. As soon as he refers to Ada, she stops prodding him with the grab-hook. But when he reverts to talking about himself, she begins to poke at him again. Paul now interprets his unbalance as a spiritual phenomenon. His unbalance is part of the life process of revolt and return from revolt which necessitates acceptance and compensation in order to achieve harmony in life.

The novella ends with Ada leaving him in the real and symbolic waiting-room, waiting for the inner strength to balance the disharmony he has just experienced. He is unsure that Ada understands him but he feels free of her and her rage and ready to face life's inevitable mysteries.

Ronald Mason finds *The Equilibriad*

uncommonly stimulating, not only for . . . technique but for the evidence . . . [it provides] of that balanced view of life—that long view. . . . *The Equilibriad* . . . is a study of rare subtlety and originality in which man is not longer seen as in conflict with the impersonal forces of scientific or industrial development, but in his even more tragic and inconclusive conflict with the evasions and ambiguities of his own nature.[25]

Paul, like the cleaner in "The Cleaner's Story" and Fireman Flower, eventually comes to face himself with a realization that both illusion and reality are at work within him. But unlike Fireman Flower and the other protagonists of the early short stories, Paul and the cleaner experience concrete turmoil that allows Sansom to eliminate solemn didactic endings. In other words, his characters are now becoming more novelistically involved with each other rather than philosophically involved with the cosmos. Paul and the cleaner also represent Sansom's successful experimentation with point of view which he will perfect later in novels.

IV   Something Terrible, Something Lovely

Also published in 1948 was the collection of short stories entitled *Something Terrible, Something Lovely*. These stories continue to refine Sansom's use of point of view from unusual angles and novelistic interaction of characters with each other rather than one character in conflict with ideology or characters serving as allegories. Among the stories, I have selected three that best exemplify Sansom's craft at that time.

"The Vertical Ladder" focuses on a boy, Flegg, who accepts a dare to climb up a vertical ladder on the side of an old gasometer. As he proceeds, his fear of heights grows; he becomes a victim of vertigo. By then, his friends seem to be bodiless, with only upturned faces watching him. When he decides three-quarters of the way up to stop and descend, he hears a commotion below. He gathers the boys have removed the painter's ladder which gives access to the first rung of the vertical ladder—his only means of retreat. He decides his only alternative to falling is to make for the platform on top of the gasometer. Shivering from fright, he courageously hoists himself up, but, when he reaches the last rung, he discovers he is not on the platform, for the top rungs are missing. Sansom ends the story by abandoning Flegg as the children have done, "clinging to the last rung of the ladder, shivering and past knowing what more he could ever do. . . ."[26]

As in "Fireman Flower," Sansom creates the intensity of a particular moment of fear in Flegg. But Flegg is a young boy being challenged by a group of young boys and girls while Flower is a mature man shadow-boxing with his illusions. On Flegg's way up, Sansom makes comparisons to situations and things that impress the boy in his growing vertigo. He screws "his eyes to any fault in the iron rungs reaching innumerably and indistinctly, like the dizzying strata of a zip, to the summit platform";[27] "the image of the gasometer became so clear that he could see the sheets of iron buckling and folding like cloth as the huge weight sank to the earth";[28] "his arms revolted at the strain of their familiar angle, as though they were flies' feet denying all natural laws";[29] or he works "his knees and elbows outwards like a frog."[30] The higher Flegg goes, the more defenseless he becomes, just as individuals feel when they are removed from the familiar sights and routines of ordinary life. The boy becomes like one of Grandville's sketches—more insect or animal than human. Sansom leaves him in a difficult situation which will require more than a child's or animal's ability to solve. Thus Flegg appears to be departing from the games of childhood to the problems of adult life. The nonverbal manner in which he realizes this is an achievement of Sansom's.

"Difficulty with a Bouquet" is a short, simple story of a man named Seal who is in his garden, overwhelmed by the beauty of the day, and inspired to pick a bouquet of flowers to give Miss D, a neighbor. But after he has gathered the bouquet his generous impulse dissipates under the self-conscious thoughts that his innocent gift might be regarded as affectation. He drops the flowers into the gutter and returns to his garden while Miss D watches from her lonely room.

She, in turn, is upset at the waste and wishes he had picked them for her. But, on second thought, she becomes as self-conscious as Seal when she realizes that she would have had to thank him. She would have been too embarrassed to talk, realizing that his tendering the bouquet would not have been a serious romantic gesture but a casual one.

Both characters reveal their isolation and fear of being misunderstood. Sansom handles the point of view of each with a perceptive "inner eye." In future collections he will enlarge on his ability to fictionalize various characters' reactions to contretemps occurring in the story.

The title story of the collection, "Something Terrible, Something Lovely," combines the child's point of view, as seen in "The Vertical Ladder," and the excitement of two characters reacting to a situation. The language is suspenseful and evocative of childhood. It successfully transforms something terrible into something lovely.

The story begins ominously as a special day brings suspense into the lives of two little girls, Nita and Dody, Nita's younger cousin.

The day slate-dark, the air still, the cindertrack by the cottages empty and without life in a watered middle-daylight—and young Nita came running, running home from school. Her satchel swung behind her, the blue exercise book fluttered its white leaves in her windmill hand, thin long legs and young-boned knees pranced before her like the separate legs of a pony careening the rest of her along. High on the brow of the slope that led down to the cottages she was already singing it out: "Dody! Dody!" so that her young voice shrill with life and so excited echoed round the black cindered emptiness of that path, sang in and out of the bricked cottage yards, rained against blind windows, rose and died with the tops of the green elms above the grey roofs, above the smoke that seemed to smell of cooked meat and coal.[31]

The gray setting and still air are animated by Nita's voice and movement. The singing quality of the passage conveys her sing-song voice and excitement. The secret she can hardly wait to whisper in Dody's ear is not revealed to the reader until the end of the story. But the unmentionable word that Nita has seen written somewhere, which she calls "the lovely terrible thing," demands a plan of action.

As the girls reveal that it was a boy who did "it" and they will do it back on the boys, the tension mounts. It mounts always from the point of view of an innocent trying to be clever but actually being melodramatic.

Their plan of action calls for the expenditure of a whole penny on chalk the next day. While they try to fall asleep, Dody casually asks Nita if she loves Stan. Nita blushes in the dark and denies it.

The next day, they surreptitiously buy white and yellow chalk. Then they seek out a tall hospital wall. The two messages they chalk on the wall climax the tension of the story while preserving the refreshing point of view of the children.

> . . . On the wall, intimately lonely among the greater loneliness of the weather and that wide vacant space, there could be read two messages written in chalk, white on the purple brick, spidery and scrawled straight capital letters, words that looked bare and cold out there in the open:
> NITA HOBBS LOVES STAN CHUTER
> A long chalk line had been drawn through this, and underneath was written emphatically, with yellow first letters to each word:
> THE PERSON WHO WROTE THIS IS DAFT.[32]

The children's naiveté and irrepressible spirit against the bleak weather provide humor and sweet revenge. In later stories Sansom will return to the theme of revenge. But the revenge will belong to childish adults, not charming children.

From Sansom's early work we can see his preoccupation with moments of intensity or revelation rather than with building up a character or plot. His characters' revelations are neither political, social, nor psychological. Rather, they are philosophical and aesthetic: philosophical when they search for the meaning of life in fires, mazes, lighthouses, and space and aesthetic when they rearrange vision, either inner or outer vision, to color a mood or emotion.

While most critics have called these earliest stories Kafkaesque, I feel they are most strongly influenced by Poe. Sansom had read all of Poe at an early age and in 1948 wrote an essay on Poe that was published first in *Penguin New Writing*, then as an introduction to *The Tell-Tale Heart: Stories by E. A. Poe* published by John Lehmann, and finally as part of a collection of essays published in 1953 in *Pleasures Strange and Simple*. The characteristics that Sansom admired the most were Poe's "strange sensibility, doomed and delighting in doom," his characters' "macabre possession," his embarkation "from a material scene of some sort—a desolate gothic manor, a torchlit immurement, a sea of polar ice—upon which his sense would play and improvise their excitations with a phenomenal intensity," his themes based on "death and stages in the decomposition of human flesh, exquisite landscapes of fantastic and more than real beauty," his passion "for explaining the mystery of life" through both intellectual solution and sensuous depths of the spirit, and, above all, his preoccupation with a spirit that resists death, making "the appearance of death itself . . . illusory."[33] These characteristics are to some extent evident in Sansom's earliest stories. They will be modified in later stories and novels by a characteristic Poe lacked—a sense of humor. Sansom's humor will emerge and his fascination with daimonic possession will fade into fascination with obsessions common to most men and women.

In stories subsequent to the collection of *Fireman Flower* we can see a tendency away from allegory and Kafkaesque nightmare toward realism achieved through a cumulation of pictures or synesthesia. We also see his increasing control over more than one character. What he has not developed here, but will in novel form, is the ability to use setting in plot and to sustain plot through intrigue and suspense.

CHAPTER 3

The Novels

IN the three decades following Sansom's first literary successes, he wrote nine novels and innumerable short stories and essays. The novels, more so than the shorter works, increasingly dealt with popular culture and the emotional issues of aging. They rarely were concerned with the turbulent political scene in Britain that evolved from postwar recession and the Welfare State. They always were concerned with characters' perception of illusion and reality in the tradition of the characters from the novels of Henry James and Elizabeth Bowen.

I The Body

The Body recounts the jealousy of a middle-aged barber, Henry Bishop, for Charley Diver, a new neighbor, who Henry believes is in love with his wife, Madge Bishop. In the tradition of Henry James and Elizabeth Bowen, Sansom structures his novel around Henry's narrow understanding of people and events. He distorts every act of his wife into infidelity and every act of Charley into lechery. They are guilty until some force from the outside can convince Henry they are really innocent.

Walter Allen in *The Modern Novel* says of *The Body*,

It is . . . a comedy of exacerbation in which the distorted vision of the hero-narrator is expressed mainly through a minute rendering of the objects that make up the external world. They are seen in an unusual clarity, magnified as though through an eye that is not a human eye. One cannot quite speak of these objects—flies, plants, the interiors of saloons, river scenes—as the background of the novel, since the human beings in it are seen in the same way and are transformed into objects also, so that they tend to merge into and become part of the fabric of things. The result suggests the literary equivalent of paintings Rousseau might have made had he been turned loose in London immediately after the war.[1]

37

While much of Allen's interpretation of Sansom's method is valid, particularly his interpretation of "the eye that is not a human eye" but an inner eye, his comparing the novel to the paintings of Rousseau is debatable. Comparing them to the paintings of Dali would have been more understandable because Sansom aims at creating not a primitive scene but a surrealistic one. Perhaps Allen is alluding more to Rousseau's naiveté than his primitivism. If so, he is not considering that Henry's naiveté, as dramatized through his perception of things, people, and events, is being filtered through Sansom's sophisticated point of view.

In the opening scene, Henry is working in his garden. With a syringe of insect repellent, he is killing a fly on a leaf.

To hold the syringe gently, firmly but delicately—not to squirt, but to prod the sleeper into wakefulness with the nozzle, taking care to start no abrupt flight of fear. Only to stir a movement, to initiate a presence from such a deep dead sleep. Gently, gently—lean thus into the ivy, face close in to the leaves, bowed in yet hardly daring to breathe, not to shake a single leaf, hand held far away up the wall, but face now close, secret, smelling the earth underneath the ivy like a smell close to earlier days, intimate the eye and closed the world . . . then carefully prod, no tickle—tickle the long-dead leg on the leaf.[2]

This ordinary act of gardening is charged with sexual connotations. The syringe that Henry holds firmly gently dispenses its venom; thus, an analogy is established to the innocent Charley Diver as a dead fly.

Once Henry kills the fly, he plays with it. Michel-Michot says,

. . . [This] gives a twofold view of Henry which reveals his motives: this infantile and perverted play with the fly, he torments in a pseudo-scientific way, has an obsessional characteristic. His acting in secret, his sense of doing something forbidden . . . [his] position . . . cannot but have sexual connotations.[3]

While he is doing this, he spies a man—Charley—red-faced and red-mustached—staring at the bathroom window where Madge is washing. From that point on, Henry fabulates an affair between the two even though Madge appears as totally innocent. Every gesture, every word, and every look of either Charley or Madge, he interprets as traitorous to his marriage. For example, Charley's red face is associated with a guilty sense of shame while his red mustache is associated to Mephistopheles. When Charley appears to blow a kiss to the window where Madge is, Henry notes that Charley is wiping the back of his hand across his mouth as if to disguise the kiss. The reader is offered an alternative interpretation to the act Henry finds so incriminating. Charley may not be, after all, blowing a kiss but merely wiping his lips on his hand. Later, when Henry and Madge are preparing to go to Charley's for drinks, Henry interprets Madge's slamming the windows shut as impatience to be with Diver rather than annoyance at his dawdling.

With every scene, Henry's anxiety and chagrin mount. John Woodburn calls Henry an Othello and says Sansom's major technique is showing how every word and gesture contains a double meaning to the jealous voyeur.[4] This technique of creating double meanings for both Henry and the reader mades the novel a tour de force.

II   *Henry Bishop*

Henry Bishop as a barber is sensitive to shapes and colors. He is also restricted by his middle-class taste and, in a perverse way, his need for melodrama in his life.

When his wife is gone from the house for two hours, he proceeds to snoop around the rooms for clues to her infidelity. First he enters his "library," which Madge calls a "den." He cleans out the drawers of his desk and locks each one, though nothing of particular importance is contained in them.

Next, he enters his wife's bedroom.

Pale blue was Madge's colour—since Father died, this was one of the first rooms she had redecorated: with the blue went a cream wallpaper and a peach-coloured carpet. Over these colours there hung a faint perfume, a pinkish-white Englishwoman's perfume of fresh flowers, a powdery smell. Dry now as the silence.

I always felt awkward in that room. Too large, too male in my dark clothes against such female tricks.[5]

Having established himself as an intruder and convinced himself of the mystery in familiar surroundings, he rifles through his wife's bureau drawers, locked lacquer box, and diary. His guilt over being a voyeur engulfs him when he hears a creaking noise from the kitchen. To his relief, he finds it is a cupboard door swinging and creaking. Sansom's humor emerges in this scene of discovery.

I paused by the door, looked through the crack—there would be a shadow if somebody was standing behind. But it showed light through. Then I caught myself crouching, felt stupid—the householder!—and irritated walked straight into the kitchen. A scullery cloth flapped—and I saw that the back door was open. That was all. Then I sniffed. There was a faint smell of pipe tobacco on the air.

I caught it again—and then it was gone. I remember walking round sniffing; but the smell was gone. Had I ever smelt it?[6]

No sooner does he quell his suspicions of an intruder than he opens up another area of suspicion by sniffing the air. His wish to catch Diver is so strong that he directs his senses to indict Diver.

Even while making love to his wife, Henry finds himself fantasizing how Diver would touch Madge in the dark. Michel-Michot says, "Henry has affection and tenderness for his wife, never love and passion. This . . . together with his absurd baby-talk with his wife, who is often presented as a kind of motherly doll, reinforces the sense of mother fixation we get, his incapacity to outgrow his childhood and his nostalgia for the past."[7]

Coupled with his nostalgia for the past is a wish to be a young man again, competing with other young men such as Charley Diver and his friends. After his ruse of going out of town on a business trip and then returning early to surprise his wife with her lover fails, he decides to give a boating party. He invites Charley, his young friends, Norma, a young woman who lives in their house, and Mrs. Lawlor, their alcoholic landlady. Even though they are all suspicious about Henry's strange prowling about Charley's flat, they accept.

III   *The Obtrusion of Reality*

The scene on the banks of a river where the boating party meets, breaks into small groups, rows, picnics, and wanders around the woods is comparable to the climax in Jane Austen's *Emma* at Boxhill. Everyone's guard is down but Henry's. While Charley playfully puts his arm around Madge's neck and a friend calls them lovebirds, Henry suffers. Then Charley performs card tricks and Madge's shrill laughter spurs him on. Henry decides on a new approach: to make Charley an intimate friend.

Later in a pub, where Henry pays for drinks for everyone, he finds he can now think of Diver in three separate ways: as a pleasant drinking companion, an old enemy he has no wish to fight, and as a new figure in an exciting intrigue. He enjoys the masochistic thoughts of Charley, his wife's lover, as his friend causing him injustice and torment. When he actually sees Diver kiss Madge and hears her laugh in enjoyment, he decides to avenge his honor.

First, he absents himself from home overnight and goes to Paliakoff's School of Gymnastics—"Be Twice the Man you are in Half the time."[8] But his wish to master a quick course in physical assertiveness fades when he sees students working out on parallel bars and with boxing gloves.

In despair he leaves the school and walks for miles. Then he stops at a pub and drinks a lot. His moment of inspiration for revenge occurs in a public lavatory. In the midst of pipes and plumbing, he remembers Diver's fish tanks. This gives him an idea.

Galvanized for the first time to go on the offense rather than passively spy and fume, he feels faint in front of a window of dentures. The effects Sansom achieves in this scene are surrealistic.

Mounted on shelves of black plywood the dentures sat and grinned. Each was isolated, crouched like a crab with indrawn legs. White pelleted teeth and harsh pink vulcanite. Secretive glints of steel and gold. Three small green cactus in pots lent their unearthly festivity, false as the teeth. White cards aggressive with black hand-penned script appealed and warned: Instead of using Powdered Glue—*Why Not Have Your Dentures Tightened? . . . A Duplicate Set in Plastic Vulcanite and Stainless Steel? . . .*
My teeth were yellow and long and now coated with stale morning. Was I old, was I dropping? I had no sharp white enamelled clenchers like these here, teeth of the strong and young and white, potent teeth. Could I have these yellow ones out, surgically drawn, and smile with bright young bone again, flash potent messages to all? Would I love Madge? Would she me? More? What are those teeth of great Diver? Strong teeth? Flesh biters? The fortunate, the giant, the fearless, the ginger. Was there no doubt but that his teeth looked white only by dint of the strong ginger moustache above them and the red beer-blue flesh that bristled purpling round them?[9]

His fantasy of Diver's young brutishness feeds into his feeling of having been sinned against. With new strength he wanders the streets of Claverton, a suburb of London.

The next morning, he awakens in the Claverton Hotel, obsessing about possible sexual scenes between Diver and Madge. By nightfall he has worked up enough fervor to go to a pub near his home and announce to all that he is a cuckold. From there he visits Charley's flat where no one is home.

It is the sight of Charley's fish tank—of the nervous glint of moving fish—that enrages him. He grabs a red hot poker and smashes the glass tank. He reports the events as if it were happening to someone else.

A fish fluttered wetly in the light—I raised my foot to stamp—then stopped, and that neighing like a guttural machine slowed and lowered itself gurgling and droning down into a long cough, a drawn staccato of deep coughing sobs. From deep inside my coat the sobs seemed to come, from the breast there, from the deepest tired layers they came coughing up like slow bubbles of air released from the blackest depth. . . .[10]

The purging of his anger by means of fishy water leaves him vulnerable to his wife's voice of calm reason. She chastises him for his sick jealousy and informs him Charley is in the hospital after an automobile accident in which a young woman friend died. The emotion of this climactic scene recedes with Henry's acknowledgment of his sick suspicions. He appears to be genuinely grateful to Madge for being so understanding.

Reviews of *The Body* were laudatory. Sansom was greeted as a fresh talent on the postwar scene. Only one critic, Frederick R. Karl, criticized this study of middle-aged frustration for stressing details at the expense of the whole. He felt that Sansom's skill in handling details was vitiated by the shallow character of Henry.[11]

I feel Sansom explored the nightmare world of an overtly shallow character with the aim of revealing what lies under the dull, normal life of a suburban bourgeois. Henry's anxieties over age, sex, and strength are eloquently described. Obsessional thinking in fiction has rarely been detailed with such intense language and imagery.

IV   *The Novels of the 1950s*

In contrast with the surrealism of *The Body*, Sansom's next two novels, *The Face of Innocence* and *A Bed of Roses*, turned to romance, comic overtones, involutions of love and marriage, and exotic places such as southern France, North Africa, and Spain. At the same time he refined his travel stories by creating plots with characters against different cultures. He tried to deepen his characterizations by dealing with psychopathic personalities, liars, kleptomaniacs, paranoids, and egotists who disrupt the lives of ordinary people in devious ways.

V The Face of Innocence *(1951)*

Two years after *The Body*, Sansom's second novel, *The Face of Innocence*, was published. It began and ended in London but ranged through the South of France and North Africa. These settings afforded Sansom many opportunities to write of the senses while depicting characters in unfamiliar surroundings. While the novel has basically the point of view of a subjective narrator, he remains nameless and, unlike Henry Bishop, is not the protagonist. He recounts the marital difficulties between his old friend, Harry Camberly, and his lovely wife, Eve, who is a compulsive liar.

Why Eve lies and the difficulties her lies cause provide the major focus of the novel. Eve fabricates "tall tales" in order to give herself an exciting past life. Harry loves her for herself and does not need the lies that she calls "dreams." In fact, it is his love that sustains her and enlists the help of the narrator to keep her from destroying their marriage. But Eve cannot settle down into marriage until she has lived out her girlish fantasy: she must have a love affair with a Frenchman, find it as hopeless as Tristan and Isolde's love, conceive a child by him, and repent. Only until she has accomplished these things can she abandon her life of lies.

VI *The Central Flaw: The Compulsive Liar*

Sansom has written elsewhere about the basis for the character of Eve. She is a composite of three women he knew, all of whom were compulsive liars.

Woman number one used to tell me in great detail about the foreign places she had visited. I was feasted with hours of mimosa and swaying palms, pink houses round perpetually blue bays, sands of languor, a sun of gold. . . . She went into carefully credible detail: sitting in the shade not of an olive tree but of a line of dreary washing; and "Can't stand the Mediterranean fish, all bones."[12]

Later he discovered that she had scarcely been outside of London. She had learned all that information from books. When he faced her with it, she dismissed the fantasy as if it had been someone else's. Nevertheless, when Sansom asked her what in the whole world she would like most, she gave the curious answer that she would most like to be seasick. This was a pathetic acknowledgment that she had never crossed the English Channel.

The second woman . . . had an unused diary from the year before on her desk. I happened to notice this . . . unknown to her. A day or two later, very nonchalantly, she began to talk of the previous year. "What a red-letter year" and so forth. And to prove it she tossed me over the diary. Every single day was filled in! . . . here were dates at the Ritz, weekends at manors, nights at glossy clubs, larded with a succession of men's names cleverly realized from a down-to-earth John to an atmospheric Guiliano. What a fascinating time she must have had—I mean, writing up the diary.[13]

He felt both sad for her and apologetic for prying into others' papers. However, he feels a novelist must be a private detective so that prying is justified as a means to the end of his craft.

The third woman not only lied about similar happenings of romantic fantasy but she also stole small objects—cigarette lighters, money from her family and friends—and she would force the gas meter or take money left for the milkman. When asked why she did this, considering that her family and friends would have lent her the money willingly, she replied that "borrowing money involved so much explanation, pleading, possible reproach."[14] Instead, she preferred the intrigue of lying, which became a form of lying to herself. Like Eve Camberly, she became so used to lying for protective or guilt reasons that it turned habitual in every small matter.

VII   The Face of Innocence *Contrasted with* The Body

The asphyxiating jealousy of Henry Bishop in *The Body* rendered through his subjective point of view as he tests reality and deduces wrongly prepares us for the disjointed world of Eve Camberly in Sansom's second novel. But *The Face of Innocence*, with its detached narrator, a novelist by profession, tells the story from the outside. This does not build tension as in *The Body*. The narrator turns himself into a spy to help Harry sort out Eve's fantasies from reality. But we never get to know Eve from her stream-of-consciousness as we do Henry Bishop. Perhaps this is one reason why his second novel is weaker. Harry and the narrator tell each other about Eve's behavior and root out the lies, but her need for creating them is never seen from her point of view.

At times the narrator of *The Face of Innocence* relinquishes the point of view to others. When Roddy, an acquaintance of Eve, takes over, he supplies confirmation of Eve's need to lie about her lowly origin and boring life. When Harry takes over, he voices a more tolerant view of her lying. Unlike Roddy, he loves Eve even for her need to create mystery about herself.

While both *The Face of Innocence* and *The Body* dwell on the divided self, the main narrator presents the problem of Eve's divided self as something to be explored rather than as a mystery to be solved, as in Henry Bishop's story. Yet, the case-history method Sansom employs in the former novel makes the reader and the narrator feel detached while the subjective first-person point of view of the latter novel involves the reader. Henry Bishop, though sick and perverted, involves the reader in the trap he clumsily sets for his wife and Diver. But the discovery of Eve's infidelity and exploits in the South of France and Tunisia does not affect the reader in the same way. The distortion of Eve's judgment does not involve the reader as Henry Bishop's distortions do.

Even the tag names Sansom chooses for each protagonist affect the reader differently. Henry Bishop's sanctimoniousness, suggested by the name of Bishop, is mocked throughout *The Body* while Eve's deviousness, suggested by the name of Eve, is compiled in an exasperated tone by the narrator. Evidently Sansom is better able to deal with awkward and often taboo topics under the cover of laughter than under the cover of a psychology.

VIII   *Eve Camberly*

In the beginning, Eve is introduced as the smiling, chic half of a charming couple, the Harry Camberlys. Then the narrator, a friend of Harry, describes in a flashback his first meeting with her four years ago. At that time, Harry was looking forward to his marriage to Eve. He called her the most beautiful girl in the world and talked vaguely about her career as a London fashion photographer's model. He also said she had had some experience with travel and men, but her past did not interest him.

But Eve's past does interest the narrator. Upon meeting her for the first time, he becomes wary when Eve calls him Harry's best friend rather than an old friend. Not only do her distortions interest him but also her past. She tells him about her first lover, Eric, a pilot who died romantically in an airplane crash, and about a subsequent lover who carried her off to the South of France but neglected to tell her he was already married.

The narrator is disappointed in her banal stories but charmed by her sincerity. He becomes alarmed, though, at Eve's attempt to draw him into conspiracy when Harry telephones and Eve motions that he is not to say she is there.

The narrator begins to count her lies—big and small—when he learns that Eve is upset over Harry's wanting to vacation on the Riviera. She fabulates a story about having had her passport confiscated once. But Harry realizes it is a lie and proceeds to marry her, get her a passport, and plan the trip abroad to include the narrator.

Even after her marriage, Eve persists in creating mystery about her past. Harry suspects she is seeing another man and asks the narrator to follow her. To his amazement, he spies her in a Chelsea tea room sitting alone for two hours and then leaving to await Harry in front of the same huge house on Cheyne Walk that he had dropped her off at earlier. Later when she insists she must go to a funeral, Harry and the narrator accompany her. They never find out whether the dead person is anyone she knows. But she weeps a lot.

Sansom has nicely translated a case study of a pathological liar into a real woman who is charming, insecure, snobbish, unfulfilled, and victimized by romantic banalities. By depicting her helpless victims— Harry, the Narrator, and eventually her baby, Miles George, Sansom shows Eve's real mystery. Diagnosis of her ills by her victims is never enough. Eve appears to be comfortable only in her fantasies, and thus she requires continual understanding and continual vigilance. She does not create these lies as a rejection of Harry and the comfortable suburban existence he offers her. Rather, she creates the lies of a glamorous past to feed her own inner hunger.

When she is honest and clear-headed about her fantasies, she is entirely pitiful. She admits she never knew her father and her mother didn't seem to, either. In her eyes, her past is tainted by the question of the legitimacy of her birth and this accounts for her snobbishness. Yet running away from home may be construed as a courageous act or even an ambitious one, not an act of cowardice at acknowledging her identity.

Perhaps the saddest passage is when Eve admits that Eric was no romantic airman but a cad who seduced her in the front seat of his car. The next moment a dream came into her voice:

"But I did love him . . . and it could have been wonderful. . . ."

Her voice was lost music. It murmured the music we think must come only with middle age—the music, the feeling that often we forget the young have too, music that breaks our hearts and sings only one refrain: "All over, all over." For Eve—yet young, yet beautiful—a part of life had already been over a long time.[15]

Thus, Sansom demonstrates Eve's ambivalence over fantasy and reality. When the narrator puts his arm around her shoulders to comfort her, she becomes hysterical. He slaps her to get her back to reality. This evokes an outburst of rage at him which ends shortly after in a serious suicide attempt by Eve. Her suicide attempt suggests that her hatred is not for the narrator, who accepts her pathology, but for herself. She despairs over ever being able to face life honestly without twisting its meaning.

IX   *The Role of Love in* The Face of Innocence

Harry Camberly, for all his seeming laconic nature, loves Eve fiercely. He accepts her boring fantasies. He has not fallen in love with her because of them. He is stalwart even in the face of Eve's extramarital relationship with the French pilot, Georges.

In fact, he accepts Eve's lies not as deliberate pathology but as philosophy. Sansom has created an interesting character in Harry although Harry in his own way is as romantic as Eve. Harry has come to terms with Eve's lying by realizing that he can never discuss past, present, or future with her, trust her when she says she is going someplace, or plan a weekend without her wrecking it. Yet he loves her just as she is, unconditionally. His major concern is for the pride she feels about her secrecy and the humiliation she will feel upon being found out. To this sensitivity, Eve never seems to reciprocate. Therefore Harry seems to be fulfilling his own image of a romantic knight who selflessly aids his lady in distress.

An additional concern of Harry's reveals some philosophical distinctions he (or Sansom) makes between the nature of the mind and the nature of reality. Harry says,

". . . I don't know whether in the end she's not right. I'm sure she half believes in all this herself. She lives in a world of what-do-you-call-it—make-believe—and I offer what I believe is reality. But what is reality? How do I know . . . that what I believe in, or do, is real? Hell, you see illusion all the time. You see an old sailor's eyes light up when he hears the pipe—and it's a damn silly sound—of a boatswain's whistle. You see a chap knocking on the door of his boss's office—frightened to death. You see an old girl in a new hat. All of them, they're believing in something quite unreal—but you can see by their faces they think it's real enough themselves. They're away in a dream of one sort or another. Ship, office, door, they are all real in one sense: in the sense that you can touch them—though I've heard even that doubted. But what the people *think* is quite different. All of those three live in two ways, they can all go about doing things practically; yet still they'll be thinking in an unreal way. It's the same with Eve."[16]

Here is a return to the early Sansom of fireman stories; here is a concern with the philosophical duality of existence which John Vickery identifies as a characteristic of a European writer rather than of an English writer. Vickery feels that English and American writers concern themselves mainly with overlapping areas of social and individual morality. He says,

> ... [Sansom dwells mainly on the intrapsychic effects] caused by time, perception, consciousness, the emotions, authority and the individual, such as perfection, and relations such as sameness and difference. . . . Sansom's philosophic problems are generated by his attraction to two questions: the nature of the mind and the nature of reality.[17]

Sansom brings about the birth of reality in *The Face of Innocence* by mating imagination and will in Harry's conviction that he has no reason to disabuse Eve of her dream.

The narrator plays the devil's advocate. He contends that Harry is wrong to suffer in peace and accept the fact that Eve will not grow up and be a sensible woman. The narrator argues that there are degrees of illusion and Eve suffers from a greater degree than most. He says,

If you want any yardstick—as to what is bad or good—you can only relate it to other people. It's finally a social question. Same with all fantasy. If an illusion injures the society around it, then it must be right. By right I mean sorted towards whatever illusion the society itself indulges in.[18]

But Harry is unmoved. His love knows no yardsticks; he accepts Eve as she is.

Harry's powerful love appears to be Eve's salvation. After Miles George is born, Harry accepts the child as his. Eve then unburdens herself in a rare moment of confession. She confesses that she tried to abort the Frenchman's child and that Georges had tired of her and found another woman. She did not blame him. When she met him to tell him she didn't love him anymore, she was impressed by the look of relief on his face.

The only humor in the novel comes at the end. There is a double turning of the tables. First, Eve for the first time asks the narrator a question about himself. He is a writer by profession. She asks, "Do you do it on a typewriter or with a, you know, a pen . . . ?"

He looks her straight in the eye and gives her back her own by lying, "On a typewriter."[19] Just as she used to lie to him about important issues, he now lies to her about minor issues. In future novels, Sansom will gradually blend more humor into the dialogue and irony into the endings just as he was doing in the short stories he was writing concommitantly to the novels.

The ending also ends the narrator's quest for truth. Like the characters in an Ibsen play, he realizes that truth may wreak disaster, as in Eve's suicide attempt. Men and women need some illusion for survival, and he now realizes Harry was right in understanding Eve's need for illusion. He no longer condemns her for lying.

Michel-Michot criticizes Sansom's use of the point of view of not only the narrator but two other characters. She says,

> . . . Sansom fails to exploit this approach so that what the narrator presents as a problem to be explored is rather treated as a mystery to be solved. Sansom has no firm grasp on his theme, and the narrator, who thinks he is endowed with psychological insight, reminds us of Somerset Maugham's stolid—I—narrators.[20]

While she is correct in her criticism of the weakness of the shared point of view, she is wrong in thinking that treatment of the problem as a mystery is a weakness. In fact, the novel would have been stronger had the mystery been exploited *more*. Telling the reader that Eve is a compulsive liar almost from the beginning throws away some of the suspense that could have been created in the characters' attempts at solving the disparities between Eve's stories and facts. In contrast, *The Body* was more effective because Sansom did not tell us Henry was jealous, he *showed* it.

As for the style, Sansom shows once again his feeling for words and the balance and rhythm of paragraphs. But he does not integrate the style sufficiently into the structure of the novel. Unfortunately his next novel, *A Bed of Roses*, does not improve this weakness.

X   A Bed of Roses

After handling complex characters in crises in his first two novels, Sansom turned to romantic comedy in 1954. *A Bed of Roses* contains the influence of the many short travel stories he was writing between novels; the setting shifts from London to a cruise ship in the Mediterranean to places in southern Spain.

Sansom gave the reason for writing *A Bed of Roses*. He was a bachelor until he was forty-two years old. By that time he had seen many friends marry. He wanted to write a story about the wrong man getting the woman in the end. But all his attempts at originality failed because of a mistake he made. He spent seven weeks touring Spain and filling notebooks with visual things. In the novel, he believed he was describing things in a bullfight, for example, that no one had ever noted before. But the result was that he focused too much on the sights and lost the narrative in the process.[21]

Perhaps another reason for his writing this novel was the unconscious influence of Jean Rhys. Sansom admired her short novels at a time when they were all out of print and she was forgotten. Rhys writes about helpless women, obsessed by love, and men who are cads. Sansom in this novel writes about Guy, a sadistic lover of Louise, who enjoys their relationship until she fights back. Also, Rhys writes from the third-person-subjective point of view, which Sansom uses in this novel unsuccessfully mainly because it is too difficult for him to adopt the female point of view. His best works are always written from the male point of view.

In the tradition of a Sansom protagonist, Louise has a flaw that prompts the action and complication of the novel. She is masochistic in her relationship with Guy, her lover of four years. Yet her masochism never reaches the dimensions of Henry Bishop's jealousy or Eve Camberly's compulsive lying. Louise does succeed in disentangling herself from her sick relationship with Guy for a little while.

The novel opens with Louise's being locked in her bedroom cupboard by Guy. He is punishing her for a minor offense—not telephoning him about her whereabouts. While she pleads and whimpers for him to unlock the cupboard, he enjoys himself destroying her most precious belongings—miniature dolls she has had since childhood.

To his surprise, destroying her childhood toys cause her to grow up quickly. She resolves to break with him and travel to Spain with her friends the Prescotts. Guy is shocked and tries in vain to apologize.

When she finds Guy on the same cruise ship, trying to make her jealous by flirting with a young girl, Molly, Louise accepts it as part of the process of curing herself of him. Within a short space of time, she meets on board a young architect, Michael Cary, to whom she becomes engaged. But she is jostled when she overhears Molly's voice in Guy's cabin. Guy, of course, has made sure that she hears him. Louise worries protectively about Molly's being taken advantage of by Guy. In her cabin she paces back and forth.

"My God, she's only a kid. She's probably half-drunk already. She doesn't know her own mind—my heaven, I'll help the little bitch . . ." and she was already patting her hair straight in the mirror, planning to go next door, pretend conviviality, pretend heaven knew what—before suddenly she felt hopeless, sat slowly down with her hands at her face knowing quite well the ambivalence of her motives. . . .
She tried to fool herself that Guy would look different, that he would be playing some special role that would alter the mannerisms she knew so well.[22]

But torn as she is for love of his face and body, she does face the facts that he cannot change his brutish disposition.

Later, when the ship lands in Gibraltar, Guy presses his fingers into her arm, bruising her as a sign of possessiveness. He also talks sarcastically, which makes him hard to accept as the charmer Sansom wishes to make him. While Guy is obviously sexually attracted to Louise, and she to him, it seems she can resist him when supported by both the Prescotts and Michael.

XI *Effect of Descriptive Setting in Spain*

The brilliantly alive setting of Spain provides an atmosphere of mounting tension as Louise and Michael vacation with the Prescotts and accidentally meet Guy. Each meeting with Guy serves to agitate Louise because she is both attracted to Guy and repelled by him.

In Seville, the air is described as being like champagne.

They walked up the plaza . . . feeling the strong distinct quality of Spain . . . the hot air that could almost be grasped in the hand, the smell of sun on old plaster, the scents of flowers and oil and havana smoke erupting, vanishing reappearing as powerfully as bars of black shadow on the hot white pavement. Tram-bells, the clatter of hooves and guttural Spanish words invigorated the ears. And for the eyes new richnesses which at first merged into a general feeling of flowers, leaves, leather, black cloth, and brass.[23]

The prose is supple and matches the movement, the relaxation, of the engaged couple just before they meet Guy again. Nevertheless, the descriptive language often goes on too long at the expense of plot.

Guy's reappearance is foreshadowed by the bull's entrance into the bullring later on the same day.

But the bull was no bull of the buttercup fields—it was bred for fighting, it was wicked and now its blood was up. And this its great defiant entrance was the zenith as the Moment of Truth would later be to the matador, of its performance. Proud, defiant, blazing angry—a proved match for lions. Yet poised there in all its black wrath, tail switching like a wild snake, hoofs pawing, it looked in that great arena most of all just lonely, a lonely giant.[24]

Guy, like a matador, talks about his admiration of brave bulls and braver matadors. He judges them like an actor, according to their performance, just as he judges his performance before Louise and her friends. Despite his exhibitionism, he is startled to hear of Louise's engagement to Michael.

Soon after, Guy tries to win Louise back. He gets into a fight with Michael. Michael is hurt and taken to the hospital.

When Michael regains consciousness in the hospital, he fantasizes that he overhears voices implying that the fight has made him impotent. After he breaks his engagement with Louise, she returns to the hotel to pack. The view from her window is described in anthropomorphic terms.

There, for the last time, lay the wide old Plaza Nueva. Feathered palms and the baroque-roofed city hall showed black against pink light rising from commercial streets beyond, and from the even greater glow that fanned out across the indigo night-sky from the distant, music-throbbing Feria. And all around rising with the scent of orange-flower and freshening leaf there sounded the love-cries of traffic, the plaintive horns honking serenade and answer, the belling of trams warm with night-blood, and the distant screech of tires as somewhere in the canyon of hidden streets a contact had been made: all swallowed in the hot heavy air, forlorn as any sound on the summer night.[25]

This description seen from Louise's point of view emphasizes the desolation she feels.

XII   *The Weaknesses of* A Bed of Roses

While the ending which brings Louise together with Guy, even after Michael learns he has not been impaired by the fight, is a surprise and contrivance, the reader is tempted to feel they deserve each other. The theme centers around the magnetism of instinctive urges such as sex, egoism, and brutishness which win out over civility and reason. The maiming of Michael suggests that Sansom intended his theme to be a serious treatment of the power of animalism over the decencies of life, but *A Bed of Roses* comes off as light romantic comedy. Louise discovers her true self not through introspection or growing sensitivity but through wandering in the scenic beauties of Spain. Michel-Michot says,

The contrast between . . . [Guy's] way of speaking and the others' is striking and illustrates the theme: the vulgar versus the conventional. It is not surprising that Louise, who speaks in the same colourless way as Molly and her friends and who is no powerful life-force herself, should eventually yield to Guy.[26]

Louise renounces the bed-of-roses life that Michael offers for the bed-of-thorns life that Guy will surely provide.

The travel-book aspect of the novel is far superior to the plot involving Louise-Guy-Michael and the subplot involving Molly and her lower-class family. *A Bed of Roses* would have been more effective as a short story. It also would have been stronger if it were not told from Louise's point of view, since Sansom is stronger when writing from a male point of view.

Sansom confessed that he found reading the criticism of this novel painful. But he said he heeded adverse criticism if it was over a page in length and represented a consensus of the critics.[27]

XIII   The Loving Eye

The Loving Eye, published in 1956, is one of Sansom's finest novels. It is redolent of *The Body* in intensity of point of view and integration of characters with setting; it reveals growth and polish in Sansom's craft. The protagonist, Matthew Ligne, is developed through the third-person-subjective point of view and the fact that he is male contributes to greater authenticity than the female point of view of his last two novels, *The Face of Innocence* and *A Bed of Roses*.

The novel is divided into two parts. The first part examines in detail Matthew Ligne's fantasy about the woman appearing at a window in the house next door. The second half examines the reality of Matthew's relationship with this woman, Lily, once he meets her.

For the most part, the narration is told from the third-person-subjective point of view of Matthew Ligne, a sick man convalescing from ulcers who sits at his bedroom window for many hours a day.

Occasionally, the narration is told from the first-person-subjective point of view of Leslie Lovelace, Matthew's companion. Leslie comments on Matthew's growing involvement with the beautiful woman at the window.

XIV   *Matthew Ligne*

Matthew Ligne is convincing as a sick man recovering from ulcers perhaps because Sansom himself had ulcers. He wrote about that experience not only in this novel but also in an excellent short story, "The Ulcerated Milkman."[28]

Matthew lives vicariously at the window of his bedroom overlooking the little gardens backed onto each other belonging to the row houses in the block. He fantasizes in particular about a new neighbor. When he sees her at her window he contrasts her favorably with the other neighbors whom he has also fantasized about. His companion-servant Leslie mocks his employer's shy voyeurism.

In the first part of the book Matthew has little direct contact with people. Only Mrs. Orme, the cleaning woman, and his eccentric old uncle come to the house. He has a polite, formal relationship with each. He is baffled by the postwar rise of the working class when he sees Mrs. Orme well dressed but working for him for low wages. Often she is called for by a friend in a larger automobile than Ligne could have afforded and she goes to cocktail parties and the theater. Similarly, his uncle, Sir Hugh, visits him because Matthew is writing a monograph on Victoria Kensington. Matthew loves tradition and the old ways. Ironically, Sir Hugh would prefer to talk about the present.

Sir Hugh was one of those energetic old men who have accepted the modern world completely. A gadget would never be new enough for him. He listened in rapture to the boom of aircraft crashing the sound barrier, his favourite walk was where yellow anti-fog lighting turned lips black and red, buses khaki, his fingers that once had savoured the finest bone china now played lovingly with the latest plastic drinking devices. He was a man of action, and loved life for itself, not for its quality.[29]

What Sir Hugh is, Matthew is not, which may account for the reason he prefers fantasizing at his window to thrusting himself on his neighbors to test his illusions. Sansom himself resembled Matthew in his love of the past. He also enjoyed working-class pubs as Matthew seems to when he visits the Goat and comments to Leslie that it used to be a footman's pub. Leslie snaps, "The past, the past, the past . . . it's like a plague with you."[30]

From his window Matthew observes his neighbors. He nicknames them Miss Tigerpants, Mrs. Peabasin, and Mrs. Average Housewife. Later on, he is shocked to learn that Mrs. Average Housewife does not conform to his stereotyped ideas.

Nor does the new woman across the way conform to his initial stereotyped idea of her. She changes gradually from a pale face with palish hair to a golden-headed girl painting her room patiently.

She held her head to one side. He knew her tongue was out—and she seemed the younger and more precious for this. Alone and hidden, and with time to spare, he felt a sudden detachment. He saw for the first time exactly who this girl was: she was the girl seen for a moment on the street, or in a bus, in the park or in the train, anywhere that made her unattainable—and is remembered forever. Her one important quality is her passing. Her merit is anonymity. If you speak to her, she vanishes, leaving someone fairly like her in her place. Either way, passing or accosted, she is unattainable.[31]

Her unattainability suits his enjoyment of romantic yearning. When Leslie invites friends to a party, Matthew prefers to leave them downstairs while he goes upstairs to watch the woman under the bare electric light of her room. There she transports him, as she would have one of Sansom's favorite writers, Marcel Proust, back to kitchens, maids, and nurses of long ago—all cosy and gentle memories. Matthew clings to his dream of her so much that he actually prays he will never meet her.

Leslie sardonically chronicles his employer's infatuation with the girl in language that differs greatly from Matthew's and contributes to the variety of Sansom's prose. Leslie narrates in mocking tones how Matthew saw a man in the woman's room who turned out to be a plumber. Then Matthew is worried about "her get-up. She looked a simple enough girl . . . then suddenly she'd come in looking like the dog's dinner, all painted up and wearing a kind of long snaky black gown, gold bangles at her throat and hair piled up like a queen. She looked ten years older. . . ."[32] Matthew becomes worried about her changed "tart-like" appearance.

Next he catches a prowler sneaking into her house and actually leaves his station to confront the man. The weapon he arms himself with is a lavatory brush. In a short humorous scene Matthew learns that the man is a neighbor seeking pleasure, not goods, from the woman. Disillusioned, he moves from the back bedroom to the front where he won't be tempted to look out the window anymore and suffer disillusionment.

In the meantime, Leslie investigates the local pub and finds that the woman of the gaudy appearance is named Dawn McGhee, an ex-pro, who is now a bar hostess. Then he clears up the mystery between the young fresh girl and aged cheap woman when he sees two women in the window. They looked the same but different, like twins that are not identical or mother and daughter or sisters in a music hall.

Finally Matthew meets the younger sister, Lily, who is working with her sister as a hostess in the Acacia Room. He comes to know her better and falls in love with the real woman. While he hates the reality of Lily, painted and dressed as a hostess while working, he is reassured by the sight in her room of a green volume of Baudelaire. For Lily, unlike Dawn, turns out to be an educated woman.

XV   *Structure of* The Loving Eye

The second half of the novel contrasts sharply with the passive observations of Matthew at his window in the first half. The pace quickens and Sansom expertly draws all the loose ends together. Lily emerges as a person in her own right. She is honest about wanting to have fun in London and fearful of using Matthew; Dawn's coarseness thickens as a reality Matthew must deal with; and the neighborhood is in a frenzy over the discovery of hacked pieces of the body of Mrs. Average Housewife buried in the garden. Sansom uses the device of juxtaposition in describing the personalities of the two sisters (Dawn is vulgar; Lily is refined); in the excitement of digging up the pieces of the murder victim with Dawn's attempt to seduce Matthew as a way of discrediting him in Lily's eyes; and in his two clumsy attempts to propose marriage to Lily.

Dawn is against Matthew as a suitor for two reasons: he is much older than Lily and he will pull her away from Dawn and the way of life she enjoys. While she accuses Matthew of "bloody baby-snatching" she also appears to be defending her own way of life.

Matthew takes this accusation with his typical love of complicating things. He rationalizes that he ought to marry Lily to get her away from Dawn's bad influence. He is unable to admit to himself a selfish interest in wanting Lily. When Matthew ponders a series of banalities about marriage, the reader will probably be bored but Sansom seems to enjoy mouthing banalities as part of the stream-of-consciousness of his characters. Unfortunately, even in a splendid novel such as *The Loving Eye*, the banalities tend to dwarf the character and make him less interesting. However, once Matthew has exhausted these banalities, he realizes that he wants to be with Lily all the time and sets about wooing her in a clumsy, complicated fashion.

Meanwhile the discovery that Mrs. Average Housewife's husband is her murderer serves both to pick up the pace of the ending and inject a note of irony on the subject of marriage. The murderer, named Mr. Mortimer, confesses that his motive for murdering her was based on his realization that they had become a banality—a smiling, happy family, as in the advertisements.

He'd look at his paper and see a smiling family there and then he'd look up slowly, just over the edge of the paper, and there sure enough was the same family smiling away fit to burst. It seems his wife's face was about the same as the kind of housewife they like to draw, and he had that clean big-jawed look, and the kids were the type too.[33]

For this reason, he killed his wife with a chopper—*"because things were too good."*[34] He couldn't bear having an illusion turn into reality, perhaps because he did not think he was worthy of such happiness. Evidently he needed to complicate his life as perversely as Matthew needed to complicate his love affair. But yet another reason may be found for this bizarre murder in the middle of a love story: it is what his good friend Mario Praz calls "a strong touch for the bizarre."[35]

Leslie reports sarcastically on Matthew's naiveté and love of complications. When Dawn lures Matthew to her room for a drink, she embraces him tightly. He feigns a coughing attack to break her embrace. But she thumps him on the back while pinioning his hands to his sides. He is too gentlemanly to voice his revulsion.

. . . He felt the soft splay of her big bosom flattened onto him and further down numberless hard knots and little corset girders as the machinery of her underdress bit into him. . . .

"Poor sweet," she cooed, but never letting him go led him to the big cushion-piled divan bed, and he had to let himself be led, only hoping when he sat down he could somehow free himself. But once down she put her head on his chest again, and now he saw a yellow-grey break in her pink hair where it parted and the rough powdered pinkness of a side of cheek and then realized her lips would be on his white collar smearing lipstick. . . ."[36]

This scene is comical even to the entrance of Lily at the wrong moment.

Matthew sets about vindicating himself. But Lily does not demand an explanation; she knows her sister's ploy. Nevertheless, Matthew takes Lily out for an evening and proposes marriage after giving her a sober accounting of his financial assets. She refuses him. While he cannot understand why, the reader does. Lily needs a more emotional and less financial argument for marriage.

At her rejection, Matthew feels his ulcer stirring and retreats to bed for days. But he cannot resist watching Lily's window. One day he purchases a bow and arrow called a Sioux Set and writes a romantic message on a piece of paper which he attaches to the arrow. When Lily's window is open, he shoots the arrow into her room.

The result is as clumsy as his first proposal. He sees the arrow hit Lily's head and then she sinks out of view to the floor. He rushes to her home and finds her stunned but unhurt. Her hat had saved her. When she sees the love message, she accepts his proposal and Dawn finally gives her blessing.

Here Sansom cannot resist adding a comic touch. "When at last they got up, straightening themselves, the tortured moan of tom-cats started from the gardens, two or three old toms must have been squatted staring at each other singing their praises. Lily laughed: "Them too," she said.[37] Then she confesses that she fell in love with him the first time they met. He is surprised that it was not when she first saw him at his window. He doesn't understand that for Lily reality is more convincing than illusion. On the other hand, she confesses that she could not accept his first proposal because it was too businesslike—too much an offer of rescue and a calculation of the chances of happiness. So, evidently, she is trying to teach Matthew how to blend the romantic aspects of illusion with reality. As in *The Face of Innocence*, Sansom is acknowledging man's need for illusion but not to the point of total distortion of reality.

XVI   *Humor in* The Loving Eye

Sansom's use of humor in the novel marks a new phase. Until this novel, he had not used the range of humor he uses in *The Loving Eye*: shift of diction, double meanings, vulgarisms, irony, parallel situations, and slapstick. For the most part, he is successful. At times, he belabors a point or dulls a situation by using clichés. At times, he bewilders the reader because the snobbishness of some characters seems more accidental than planned or depends upon knowing the English caste system that was so important to the prewar British world.

Lower-class speech is introduced in pub scenes, nightclub scenes, and anywhere that Dawn is. When she appears at the pub, the Goat, for Matthew's first close viewing of her, she cries, "Wotcher!" to the landlord and then to a man who is choking on his cigarette, "Coughing better?" In the background a young soldier is singing a ditty, "Put Away Your Tweezers Till Our Eyebrows Meet Again." Dawn is shrieking the name of her club, the Acacia Room, as Arsearsia.[38]

Later Matthew winces at Dawn's speech, though he is disapproving of his need to label it as a defect.

... His ear always reacted before his mind was brought to bear down fairly and classlessly. Dawn's were such little lapses. She pronounced "revolver" as "re-vo-o-lver," words like "ill" became "iwl," and she used "bought" for "brought" and "lay" for "lie" and so on. The very finest shade "off-colour."[39]

The murder victim, Mrs. Average Housewife, provides light, humorous touches before her disappearance. Sansom notes that clothespegs always jutted out of her mouth like comic teeth, that her face was innocent of all sensuality, that her dimples and sensible haircut merited few whistles on the street but many murmurs of approval in the launderette, and that she always sang in a cheerful soprano of a long-lost Latin love with the phrase "pining for the Argentine."[40] Ironically, her innocuous appearance and personality work against her. Her husband blamed them as the reason for his urge to murder her. He, too, provides moments of levity which resemble gallows humor. When apprehended for murder, he never shows any emotion. In fact, he has been such a good father that he put the television on for his children while he was murdering his wife so that they would not be disturbed by the fuss. Later, when in prison, he becomes very agitated over hearing that the authorities have been digging up his beloved garden in search of his wife's remains. He hollered, "What they been doing to my beans? . . . What's my marrow like?"[41] His concern is based upon his knowledge that he carefully buried the parcels of his wife's body between the roots of his vegetables so as not to disturb their growth!

An amusing scene with erotic overtones occurs when Matthew is giving a party but wants to leave it to go to his post by the window upstairs in order to watch Lily. A guest, his doctor's wife, interrupts him when she enters the bedroom to nurse her infant son.

> The woman shuffled the child up and down, the night and the baby's howling deepened.
> "It's the wind," Margot said.
> Ligne looked anxiously out of the window. "It's getting up again, is it?" The weather, somehow, had become the province of that girl at her window.
> "No, *his* little wind, silly." She banged the child down on a cushion. . . .
> "Time for his feed. You don't mind do you." Magically, part of Margot's dress fell open and a rich wealth of breast poured out, white and brown, vanilla with a coffee centre. Margot put the little old man to this, as, in nervous access, Ligne's ulcer bit him inside. Has it not been said that ulcers have little round teeth of their own and that you have to feed them? Was his then envious of the baby's good fortune?[42]

This action counterpoints Matthew's view of the woman at her window as Flaubert sets the flirtation of Emma Bovary and Count Rudolphe in *Madame Bovary* in an empty building overlooking a country fair at which heifers are being auctioned off at high prices. The seductive conversation between Emma and Rudolphe counterpoints the primitive talk of the auctioneer. But the simultaneous effect of two diverse topics, sophisticated banter and crude evaluation of animals, creates a comic situation. The healthy, animal demands of the nursing baby half succeed in diverting Matthew from his compulsion to watch his woman at the window and indulge in febrile fantasy. He yearns to be suckled tenderly and he yearns to hold the woman of his fantasy tenderly.

Through Leslie's monologues, Sansom inserts vulgarisms, anecdotes, and light jokes. He is amused at his employer's need to watch his neighbors and at his inability to act quickly with Lily once he has met her. Leslie thinks in terms of cat imagery.

> You'd think he was an old peep-bo tomming the sights again, safely stuck behind his curtain with a nice book handy. But that's not Ligne's line, you could have stripped the Queen of Sheba and thrown in Sheffield Thursday [the day for open markets in Sheffield] and he wouldn't have looked that-a-way. . . . You've got to be a window-cleaner to do the job properly, and a proper job they do from what they tell me, what with hubby at the office and the missus handing out cups of you and me with plenty of me. Home life isn't all telly, not by a long way. I know a nice young chap in the electrical line, didn't like his cup of tea, really wanted to vacuum and what does this mother-of-three do but get him the sack. Cheeked her, she said. Sweet old lady.[43]

Leslie revels in reporting that a pussy has dug up another piece of body and he likens his master to a cat on cold bricks. When Matthew is upset over Dawn's interference, he starts changing rooms around and asks Leslie to "hump" furniture for him. This is a slip of the tongue for Matthew and it seems natural.

A cat also interrupts Matthew and Lily in a passionate embrace. As they are nestled closely on a park bench, a cat rubs against Lily's legs and then jumps onto their laps. Reluctantly he strokes the cat and it purrs. Lily shoos it away and they return to their passionate embrace.

Just as Matthew gets ready to confess his love for her, the cat returns, rubbing and pressing. He cannot find the words in the presence of the rubbing cat. So, instead of proposing marriage, he proposes a job for Lily.

Later that night, as he puts out food for his own cats, he is relieved that the cat in the park interrupted him. His passion, in his opinion, had been too strong for that point in their relationship. The cat, he thought, really was not his enemy but his savior.

Leslie provides the sexual commentary that dignified, upper-class Matthew would never articulate. At times, its sexist attitude wears the reader thin. At other times, when Leslie notes the stuffiness of the upper class, he is highly amusing. Here are some of the one-liners and worn-out jokes that he delivers in the pub:

"There's you and this chap . . . [in the lavatory]. So what do you say? 'What goes in must come out' . . . [or] 'The business in hand—that's another one.' . . . What do you say if you're on a railway platform and the barometer's five below? 'Hot enough for you?' you say. And that breaks the ice nicely, thank you. Or how about when you've let fall a naughty word in front of the ladies: 'Pardon my French!' They *like* it. 'Enjoy your trip?' says a bus conductor when you fall flat on your fanny, and this particular password they also call cockney humour, *perky*, you can't keep a good cockney down. . . ."[44]

Leslie foreshadows other comic characters in future novels who will supply the low comedy while the protagonist will supply the high comedy by his innocent misunderstanding.

XVII *Sansom's Achievement*

Walter Havighurst in the *Saturday Review* admired the subtle way in which the manservant, Leslie, picked up the narrative. "Leslie's mocking tone makes a brittle counterpoint to the wistfulness and yearning of the middle-age daydream, which happily becomes reality."[45] While Matthew's problem is explored from within by his own narration, Leslie serves in his narratives to explore Matthew's problem from without.

Sansom's handling of the narrative has tightened up considerably since the subjective narration of *The Body* and diffused objective narration of *The Face of Innocence*.

Sansom has also tightened up the theme. Unlike the constant story interruptions in *A Bed of Roses*, the setting is subordinate to the action. Matthew is, at first, afraid of reality and the present. He avoids both by passively watching life go by his window and by delving into Victorian monographs for his own monograph on past beauty. When he finally meets the woman he has fantasized about, he falls in love with the reality of her. Unlike the husband of Mrs. Average Housewife who murders his wife because of boredom with perfection, Matthew does not allow himself to be bored by Lily's personality. He discovers in it a puzzling reality, not a simplistic one from the world of the media, and thus he retains the magic of things unknown which are still to be explored.

The Loving Eye also handles setting exceedingly well. Perhaps Sansom had heeded his critics of the two previous novels. David Daiches, in *The Present Age*, says that Sansom is

. . . a clever and versatile writer, who has a tendency to play tricks on the reader. His most characteristic device . . . is to incorporate stories or a novel into a travel book, as it were, where an account of human relationships is set against a carefully described topographical background. His carefully wrought prose is a considerable achievement. But his skill has still to come to terms with his imagination.[46]

From the strengths of both *The Body* and *The Loving Eye*, the topography of an unassuming London neighborhood stands out. Ordinary people fill the scene and Sansom brings both them and their background to life with the extraordinary diction in all its variety that marks the best of his fiction.

XVIII   The Cautious Heart

The firm control of point of view and theme that Sansom exhibited in *The Loving Eye* continued to strengthen in his next novel, *The Cautious Heart*, published in 1958. While the theme depicts man's pursuit of an elusive dream, his pursuit is enriched by and related to the problems raised in the contemporary world. It is a romantic comedy combined with an in-depth study of a psychopathic character named Colin who keeps the lovers apart for awhile.

The point of view is that of a musician who narrates the story from the first person. He is the protagonist and one of the most convincing of Sansom's narrators.

The narrator plays the piano at the New Marlven Club in London. While he plays, he observes the customers. He becomes interested in two customers who come in together: Colin, with the "clipped, clean-jawed, hard-bitten look of a British officer," and Marie, a "little brown mouse-woman" who pays for their drinks. The pianist then sees Colin steal a pepper-pot. After they leave, he notes that a fork and tray are no longer on their table.

It takes a few meetings for the narrator to sort out Marie's relationship with Colin. Marie assures him it is friendship, not love. Yet Colin maintains a curious hold on her. As the narrator falls in love with Marie and becomes more possessive of her, his jealousy of Colin grows. Eventually Colin becomes the major irritant in their relationship.

XIX   *The Character of Colin*

Colin's character is reminiscent of the character of Eve, the compulsive liar of *The Face of Innocence*. He lies and steals, abuses peoples' trust, and yet keeps relationships.

When the protagonist-pianist first confronts Marie with Colin's theft of things from the club she attributes it to a kind of kleptomania and a wish for a Dutch uncle. Her tolerance of Colin mystifies the protagonist. He finds himself becoming jealous of Colin's special relationship with Marie.

Later, when the protagonist meets Colin's woman friend, Eileen, his jealousy is still unallayed. Marie calls Eileen odd but good for Colin. Sansom obviously enjoys describing her oddness. She works at demonstrating products.

. . . Eileen is dressed in an emerald uniform as some superior kind of air-hostess. And from the fine brass instrument she carries, one gathers that she is the one who blows the hunting horn at the back of the aeroplane. But this is no more, on closer acquaintance, than the Ozal Gun. Under her jaunty forage-cap, Eileen is as heavily painted and luxuriously coiffeured as a professional odalisque: except that no professional, knowing that her

business is to improve upon rather than occlude Nature, would ever have
gone so far . . . a white-skinned redhead . . . stronger than any disinfectant
she might carry in her little brass fun, there hangs about her a heavy smell of
white night flowers.[47]

Eileen is firmly placed in the postwar world of public relations which
creates illusions in terms of image in advertising. This brassy
commercialism seems to both amuse and annoy Sansom, perhaps
because it does not hold any of the beauty that his illusions hold.
Nevertheless, both this novel and *The Loving Eye* pertain to
contemporary life more than any previous novel of his.

Colin hangs onto Eileen parasitically, particularly when he is broke
or between jobs, which occurs often. He also is attracted to her
because of her odor—she smells of petrol. And, Marie calmly
explains, Colin is a petrol sniffer. Although she criticizes him for
being addicted to such a second-rate drug, she accepts his weakness.

Colin then proceeds to leave the narrator to pay for their drinks
while appealing to him for a loan. The narrator lends him money,
thinking it will keep Colin from moving into Marie's flat when he is
forced to vacate his own. Marie thinks the narrator is very kind but
she warns him that Colin will never repay him.

Most of the time, Colin appears drunk and feckless. His job history
is erratic and he has even forged checks with impunity. He claims his
real profession is photography but his camera is in pawn. He is inured
to the continual crisis of being forced to leave his lodgings because he
cannot pay the rent. He usually appears smiling and talkative:
insensitive to the feelings of others and their need to work hard for the
necessities of life.

As the narrator's affair with Marie deepens, he finds himself
constantly alert to the next intrusion of Colin. While lunching with
Eileen and Colin, he finds himself envious of Colin's knowledge of
Marie.

. . . He talks of a year-ago party—from the few things he says, her image
comes to me, I see her dress, smell her powder, see her fall over, laugh as she
gets up. . . .
I hear that she is impatient in shops and always overbuys, she loves the
ugliest animals in the zoo and she has a reverence for old-fashioned
convention and manners which she never follows in practice.[48]

As Colin speaks of her, the narrator constructs his own images of his
beloved's past. He finds it hard to believe she could overbuy or have

faults. He also finds it hard to give Colin credit for sensitivity to anyone but himself.

When the narrator tries to find out why Marie allows herself to be exploited by Colin, she reluctantly explains. She feels one must help a friend in need, that she can't let him go hungry when broke, and that she would rather help him than see him go to jail. Furthermore, she admires him for his principles. He blasts plutocrats, bureaucrats, and bourgeoisie alike in a continual mad litany. What the narrator cannot understand is why Marie, knowing all Colin's weaknesses, still aids and protects him. He can only conclude she is in love with Colin. At the same time, he plots to find a job for Colin so that he can have Marie all to himself.

Eventually Colin befriends the Adrians, a nice couple who frequent the New Marlven Club. With aggressiveness, he gains their sympathy and hospitality and moves in with them for, supposedly, a short time. He says he is job-hunting but he considers most jobs beneath him. Besides, he always seems to find sources to borrow or get money.

XX   *The Holiday in the Scilly Islands*

While the narrator with his cautious heart is weighing the depth of his love and ability to cope with her parasite, Colin, Sansom is weaving a bit of his love of travel into the story. The narrator takes Marie away for a holiday in the Scilly Islands. The Scilly Islands provide Sansom with an opportunity to describe a setting that does not usually appear in fiction. Notice how he integrates the setting with the lovers' feelings of vulnerability.

The hotel, with its planked bar-room and photographs of wrecked three-masters, its white and black figurehead among veronica in a green Atlantic garden, its gull-cries down the chimney and its few flighty modern furnishings, gave us our first feelings of permanence together. . . . We have travelled from winter into spring. There is strength in the sun's warmth: sheltered from the sea-breeze behind a wall with a camelia tree glowering rose against a deep blue sky, one could imagine oneself in a draughty corner of the true South. . . . Marie . . . wore the highish heels of some kind of weather-proof boots on her sparrow feet, looked tartly out of place, as if she had been dropped from an airliner. City-bred man should always take his girl to the country: there she looks properly isolated, fresh and vulnerable, a good test for the main barometer of love, his protective instinct. Marie looked doubly vulnerable in her London clothes. . . . My own mercury showed high pressure.[49]

Thus Sansom integrates the flowering spring with the flowering love of the couple. The narrator's urge to protect her suggests a change from the old urge to protect her from Colin. Now the urge seems related to a wish to marry her.

Their idyll is broken on the second day by a letter from the Adrians. They have been robbed and the police and insurance company want Colin's address. They only want to question him about a clue—the mark of a rubber-soled shoe with the brand-name Ducksweather—found all over the house. Despite Otto Adrian's assurance that Colin could soon show his innocence by proving he had no shoes of this kind, the narrator knows differently.

Once this letter arrives and soon after Colin, who has been summoned by the protective Marie, Sansom's descriptions echo the change of mood.

The Atlantic sunset did its best to help my foreboding. A low red sun made huge by a pearled sea-mist, and the islands floated out to sea like the very end of all lost land and time, disappearing over the edge of a wet world like every other golden moment never to be regained.[50]

Once Colin arrives, by airplane rather than by the more economical boat, the couple's golden moments vanish. He has been drinking or sniffing petrol and is anxious to continue drinking.

Marie has told the narrator that she bought the Ducksweather shoes for Colin and when she sees that he is still wearing them, she exclaims,

"Good God, you've got them on!" . . .
    He looked down and laughed: "Oh, the old Duckswear? You don't expect they're going to"—and he dropped his voice to a stage whisper—"follow me *here* with their magnifying glasses?"[51]

Colin mocks their concern for his safety with a combination of lack of conscience and braggadocio. As usual, he enjoys being the cynosure of Marie's world, despite her calling him a fool.

Marie finds a French trawler to carry Colin to safety in France. But he does not wish to leave. Like a good sociopath, he believes he is untouchable by the law or anyone. In an attempt to divert him from drinking, they get him to go out on the quay and inspect the French trawler. There he shocks even Marie by pulling out of his trenchcoat a flat full bottle of whiskey and guzzling it until he can barely speak. While he takes up their time, the narrator and Marie wait for some action, knowing full well that Colin is incapable of any. Both are compassionate in this scene despite the burden Colin imposes on them.

But the affect of the compassion on the narrator is to cause him to feel the old boredom he experienced before meeting Marie. This boredom prevents him from feeling savage. He examines his condition in the manner of the characters from Sansom's early stories.

> The dullness had taken over like a protective blanket, which it might well have been. Glum thoughts revolved. . . . The only true escape from the daily round: drink, travel, hobbies are minor escapes compared with truly elevated boredom. It lowers you above *everything*. Here we have a true state of pure waiting, properly in communion with death, all life a death-wait on the start-finish *prinzip*. Like smoking a cigarette, completing a meal, going to sleep, we always want to finish things off, ourselves too. . . . I looked over at Colin almost with admiration, he really got inside one, right under your skin. . . . [52]

Like Ivan Bunin, the Russian writer (often mentioned by Sansom) who was more than half in love with death, the narrator finds solace in the feelings of futility Colin causes him to have. These feelings, channeled into boredom, prevent him from taking action. He realizes that any plans he makes, Colin will veto or subvert. But he begins to reason that the only way the police can trace Colin is through Marie. If he can separate Marie from Colin, Colin will have a reasonable chance of remaining free of the authorities.

As reasonable as his plan is, Colin is indifferent. Again, his indifference to his own safety seems related to his illness. He feels untouchable.

They all three wander aimlessly about the beach. Colin drinks more, and while Marie decides to sunbathe on the sands Colin decides to go for a swim. The narrator tries to dissuade him from swimming. In a rare moment of honesty, Colin confronts the narrator with his knowledge that the narrator wants to pull him away from Marie. He also admits he has butted into their affair and knows how the narrator feels toward Marie. This reawakens the narrator's jealousy, which he has been trying to suppress. Colin senses this and assures him that there is nothing between himself and Marie. His words soothe and an uneasy camaraderie begins between the two men. Colin goes off to swim; Marie is already lying on the beach asleep; the narrator lies down near her and falls into an uneasy sleep.

In a dream, he sees Marie ripping labels out of his clothes and exchanging them for the labels in Colin's clothes. Colin is smilingly filling the narrator's pockets with his own effects. He looks ten years younger and is wearing dark glasses. The dream has a convincing ring: the narrator is insecure and feels easily displaced. He also feels competitive with Colin but too old to keep up with such boyishness.

When the narrator awakens, he sees Marie still sleeping and Colin asleep at the edge of the water, half-naked and with a whiskey bottle clutched in his hand. Suddenly the tide rises steeply and pulls Colin's body out to sea. The narrator watches and deliberates. He can save Colin or let him drown. Certainly, his lack of presence in their lives would be a welcome event. The narrator deliberates:

> If he wakes now, he will be saved.
>
> If the water reaches no higher, he may be saved. If not—it is the law of chance.
>
> The law of chance, the suspicion of destiny, made this a fatal decision which no one could alter and upon which, lying there, I placed a careless fascination, involved as a child with whether a thing could happen or not— I'll eat my sweet when the third bus passes! I'll count a hundred before the lightning comes again! compelled and held.[53]

These childish thoughts, redolent of Sansom's naive children of the story "Something Terrible, Something Beautiful," are quickly dispelled by the adult man that he is. He dashes into the water and, after a great deal of difficulty fighting the surf and Colin's slippery body, he saves his life.

XXI   *Resolution of the Conflict*

The heroic act of the narrator which saved Colin's life appears to have thrust them all back into the same bind as before. Colin remains their problem. If they are to be together, they must all three evade the police.

But the narrator's act actually accomplishes two things. It brings him and Marie together as never before with her acknowledgment that he has acted out of humanity rather than jealousy. It also represents a new-found acceptance by the narrator of a human being who is an outcast of society. This acceptance of Colin, with all his blemishes, as an important person to Marie reveals the depth of his love for Marie.

He is astonished to find that Marie returns his love. When they go to bed that night, the narrator, with new-found consideration of Marie after the traumas of the day, distracts himself from thoughts of sex by trying to compose a lyric. There follows a humorous scene.

When you write a lyric, it is not simply a rhyming matter. You must think of the words as being sung, of the tongue and the lips, of whistling "s's" and drumbeat "d's." And of the little up and down tune that words themselves make in ordinary speech. It is not enough cleverly to rhyme "chrysanthemum" with "Iolanthe, mum." . . . I was . . . trying to translate a vapid aria in which the word Liselotte had to be rhymed—it was part of a German operetta—as will happen, the most inappropriate rhymes came idling through, "voce sotter," "got a motter," "she's a rotter." . . . Then Marie's book went down and in the same moment she had turned on her side and put her arms all around me. She said nothing but clung close kissing me—and then for some seconds it was I wearing the cold cream of my Liselottering who could not respond, but then I did, and we made love until candles would have gutted . . . as if . . . we had found each other now for the first time.[54]

He concludes in a somewhat clichéd manner afterwards, but a wholly authentic manner to the English middle-class mind of the 1950s, that he can never again pretend to know what a woman will do next. While deploring woman's inconsistencies is a popular male pastime, Sansom (or the narrator) is trying to learn the difference between male and female needs and values.

Their problem with Colin is solved when the police appear and take him off with them. On the couple's train journey home, the narrator proposes marriage and is accepted. The novel ends with the discovery that even now Colin is still with them—in another compartment with the police.

XXII   *Setting*

Sansom uses two settings at the beginning of the novel to establish the mood. They also suggest by analogy elements of the conflict that is about to break.

One setting is the New Marlvern Club. Here the narrator plays the piano in a pleasant club that caters to middle-class Londoners.

A glance round reveals a few regulars. The Adrians are nestled together turning over handfuls of jewellry in their minds. Leather-wristed Raoul sits sipping a sweet cocktail and glancing over the *Vogue* pattern book. A group of young men and their girls burst into occasional loud laughter. They seem to be on their way to a dance, the men in dark well-pressed suits, with white handkerchiefs set in breast-pocket triangles, and the girls sticking naked arms and shoulders out of tulle dresses that rob them of shape yet cloud them with freshness. . . . They all look remarkably fresh—as if they lived in rarefied air under cellophane . . . .

The fizzing of siphons, the clink of glasses, bursts of laughter, and all the murmurous mumble of voices mingling with my own soft ompety-pom, which I let fade and grow loud successively, like waves eavesdropping. Bit of fluff, smoke, ash and the smell of spirits, the muzz of noise and the little flickerings of light as rings flash, teeth smile, bodies and faces move—and this whole room vibrates with an allover presence, something not quite placeable, like the bell-hum of an aircraft on a cloudy night.[55]

Again, like Ivan Bunin, Sansom creates a paean to life in his savoring of sights, sound, and smells so that both Bunin and Sansom, though attracted to death, are also attracted to the zest of life.

The club provides an enclave for its members, a place where they can feel a sense of identity in an increasingly depersonalized world. Club life, though currently fading with the change in licensing laws, was just as strong in the 1950s, when *The Cautious Heart* was written, as before the war. The intrusion of Colin with his kleptomania and crudeness is not welcomed by the other members. But, on the basis of knowing the narrator, Colin manages to ingratiate himself.

The other setting that establishes mood is the Exhibition Hall, where Eileen demonstrates new animal products for a dog show. The Exhibition Hall demonstrates the postwar thrust of commercialism.

The enormous belly of the hall, tiered with upper floors, misted with blue smoke and the glass-domed echo of thousands talking and barking, gives the impression of a vast Assembly Room in which a hundred cock or dog fights are being held at once. In all directions separated circles of macintoshed and tweeded backs hide each particular event. Occasionally the amplifier, godlike master of ceremonies, intones a general message to hearten us; and then one imagines that everyone should change places, as in musical chairs. A smell of biscuit, sawdust and doggy fur hangs thick in the air.

We get mixed up in one of the circles. An ordinary-looking man extraordinarily briskly walks to and fro holding out at arms-length a lead with a morose-looking hound on the end of it. He walks hard across the open space towards the wall of spectators. He won't, he can't, he'll *never* stop himself—he's going straight through! . . . That man's eyes are fixed on a middle distance quite his own. He is a fanatic, a visionary. The dog, a Red Setter looks half-mad too. . . .

We press on past a row of wired hatches containing white and brown dogs with sad topheavy heads, Basset Hounds, wasserköpfen of the dog world:

past a frisk of Pomeranians: past Bedlingtons like long-legged lizards worked in wool, past a dragon display of Pekingese Terriers. Past Fox-terriers, past youth.[56]

The hall where dogs of fine breeding are being exhibited sharply contrasts with the vulgar commercial note Eileen introduces in both her merchandizing efforts and her outfit. Perhaps Sansom is also parodying the British love of animals which may be sometimes to the exclusion of human beings. The exhibitionism here is given free reign and Colin, when he appears, fits right in. The more Colin fits into an ambience, the more of an outcast the narrator feels.

The only neutral territory in the first half of the book appears to be Marie's flat, where the lovers can communicate undeterred by the decorum of the club and its self-conscious members or by the crass and primitive world of the Exhibition Hall, where dogs are displayed and humans recede into the background.

Sansom appears to be most interested in sensitive people who, despite being mocked by reality, seek order and peace. The narrator in *The Cautious Heart* avoids exploring Marie's character. He finds her elusiveness an incentive to love her more. This pursuit of an elusive dream or dream-girl is a favorite theme of Sansom's that is explored even more in short stories than in his novels. While the act of winning the girl often contains a mixed bag of reactions, winning in this novel seems a more natural turn of events. The narrator's discovery of Marie's complex and unexpected reactions helps him discover not only Colin's and Marie's natures but his own.

Colin is the catalyst for the narrator's self-knowledge. The narrator realizes that although Marie knows Colin's flaws she is ready to defend him against the world. Only by understanding this and joining forces with her in accepting Colin will he achieve her total love.

Unlike Henry Bishop of *The Body*, whose jealousy blinds him to alternate interpretations of Madge's actions, the narrator in *The Cautious Heart* fights his jealousy by constantly seeking other interpretations for Marie's actions or words. Ronald Mason, in "William Sansom," discusses this task. He says,

The moment of Sansom's imagination that saw the thing as living and the men as passive and powerless subordinates has been extended and amplified into a prime factor of his inspiration. This brilliant reversal of the design of familiar activity has determined, whether consciously or not, the form of his more important later writings.[57]

In *The Cautious Heart*, Sansom turns his narrator's powerlessness into a virtue. He wins his woman and accepts her parasite not by means of ultimatums but by means of accommodation (which was the same psychology used by powerful nations at that time—1958— in sparring over the Cold War).

The television film made from this novel was retitled "A Man on Her Back" (1966). The title represents Marie's dilemma better than that of the original title. Marie has a problem with her own generosity to Colin, ungrateful as he is, while *The Cautious Heart* implies that the narrator is wary of commitment because of his own timidity or lack of understanding.

Compared with *The Loving Eye*, *The Cautious Heart* maintains Sansom's new-found strength of characterization through reconciliation of fantasy and reality. Matthew Ligne is more passive than the narrator-pianist while Dawn is more stereotyped than Colin as the obstacle. Both Lily and Marie are depicted sketchily. They are mere foils to Dawn and Colin. Still, *The Cautious Heart* represents improvement in Sansom's style because his protagonist is more mature than Matthew and he develops more compassion in the course of the story than Matthew does.

XXIII   *The Novels of the 1960s*

The novels of the 1960s in Britain contained a wide variety of subject matter. C. P. Snow wrote of moral agnosticism, Anthony Burgess wrote of futurism, Margaret Drabble wrote of feminism, and Paul Scott wrote of the twilight of British imperialism. Their characters were professors, linguists, college-educated housewives, and military leaders. In contrast, William Sansom retreated from heavy intellectual subject matter and complex characters. While he retained his interest in illusion and reality, he no longer handled it from the point of view of an eccentric narrator. Rather he chose to examine the plastic world created by hucksters. This world sells people "new images" and "new identities." The characters who buy these illusions are ordinary people, office workers, salesmen, and white-collar workers. They are deluded by status symbols and the promise of affluence. The result is that they are masked not only to themselves but to each other. They are forever waiting to "become" someone glamorous or lovable.

XXIV   The Last Hours of Sandra Lee
Contrasted with A Bed of Roses

Against a background of depersonalized modern life, the heroine, Sandra Lee, of *The Last Hours of Sandra Lee*, published in 1961, searches for her real self and for magic during her last hours of freedom as a single woman. Like Louise in *A Bed of Roses*, Sandra fears the monotony, security, and comfort offered by her fiancé, Bun, who is about to leave England for foreign service in Sarawak. Unlike Louise, who throws away a life of ease in order to follow her animal instincts with Guy, Sandra settles for life with Bun as Marjorie, her real name, which she had cast aside in an effort to become a modern woman of the media.

XXV   *Effect of the Setting on Characters*

Sandra Lee works for a cosmetic firm, Allosol. It is an office full of ordinary routine, yet the promise of beauty that her firm produces seems to be within her reach. Except for a lunch with Nevile Wrasse, a dashing upper-class seducer, the entire action of the novel takes place in one day, mostly inside an office. It is Christmas and the office party is Sandra's last chance at a wicked adventure because the next day she is supposed to marry Bun and leave for Sarawak. As the day wears on, Sandra becomes increasingly reluctant to leave Allosol and get married.

Various characters in the office hinder or help her face this important decision. Her belief in the potential glamour of her banal office life is shaken when H.J., the boss, confides that the Christmas bonus will be less this year. He complains of the financial straits of the company while in reality he is planning on expansion. He pledges her to secrecy about the small bonus until he announces it at the party. She agrees with tears welling in her eyes, thus displaying the plastic effect big business can produce even when its intention is malevolent to the workers. Sandra appears to be more ignorant than stupid.

Jill, who works with her and is her confidante, meets Sandra in the ladies' room. It has been painted bright red by a time-motion company to encourage the women not to dally there. Sandra confesses her uncertainty about marrying Bun. She feels guilty because she refused to have lunch with him in order to have lunch with Nevile Wrasse.

While typing letters, she remembers Christmas at home with her parents as a dull routine. They all three always thought nothing much had happened in the past year. Sandra was then Marjorie, and Marjorie, she shudders to recall, spent a lonely vacation in Brittany and in Paris run away terrified at the first sight of a flirtatious man. Unlike Eve Camberly, Sandra recognizes her dull life and does not lie about it to others or herself. She also realizes that Bun is part of her past. He is dull but secure.

Although Sandra is not obsessed by jealousy, as other Sansom protagonists have been, she is not able to forget two embarrassing misadventures which she titles "The Day She Passed Out" and "The Evening with the Wigged Man." Both misadventures ended with her running away from men who seemed both worldly and frightening. The memory of them forces her to admit that she cannot live up to the daring image of herself that she often fantasizes. Her desire to be naughty and defy conventions always ends with her innate goodness and propriety taking over.

Daphne reminds her that her appearance belies her conventional values. When the office members once asked her to join in drinking at a Chemin-de-fer party, she visualized blue-uniformed figures popping in and so went home. Yet, other members of the office comment on her good qualities:

"She's the good-time-Charley type," thought Mansford, "poor Charley."

Miss Cook sometimes thought, "She's the marrying type, underneath all that mess."

"The near-delinquency type," dreamed big Hearst, in an imaginative moment, "about thirty-six-twenty-two-thirty-six."

Jill Jenkins had often paused to consider, "She's the loyal type. I'd trust her anywhere. That child's got her head screwed on all right."

"Looks a bit screwy," H.J. had once thought, "but a solid worker." And glancing up at her back as she walked off, "I wonder what it'd be like?"

"Dreamy type," Monica Naseby had once said, "airs and graces, crocodile tears, cupboard eyes, silly little cow."

A big pale-faced office boy on the floor below spent hours thinking, "Oh, darling, Sandra, look at me!"[58]

Thus Sandra's two sides confront herself and her comrades. The women judge her weakness as due to a lack of common sense while the men judge her weakness in terms of their own sexual fantasies.

On her luncheon date with Nevile Wrasse she allows him to buy her a dress to replace the one she has just ruined in the office. When Sandra first learns that he has charged the dress to his mother's account, she feels insulted. But soon she changes her mind and feels delighted at the thought that she appears to be a wicked, "kept" woman. Neville is a stereotyped roué. He orders oysters for their supposed aphrodisiac effect. Then he orders steak for two to suggest to her the intimacy he anticipates sometime after the meal. As he eats, his eyes devour her smooth-skinned arms. Yet, when he suggests meeting Sandra after the office party that evening, she demurs. Through conversation with him, she realizes she not only does not know herself but also does not know the people with whom she works.

XXVI   *Bun Stanbetter*

Perhaps because the novel is seen through the point of view of Sandra Lee, her fiancé, Bun Stanbetter, is depicted as a stereotyped young man. He is trusting, patient, masculine, and, above all, undeterred by all the real and imagined obstacles Sandra Lee natters about. He is depicted mostly on the telephone, frantically trying to meet Sandra, or at a clinic, having shots, or at the door of the office, being misled. He is a typical Sansom-male character in his despair over the fussy things Sandra wants. Obviously he will be the man to tame her.

At one point in the day, Bun visits Sandra at the office to convince her to marry him immediately because he is leaving for Sarawak the next day. She would like to postpone that decision and have a last fling. He is bewildered by her hesitation. She claims she owes Allosol loyalty and more notice that she will leave. He says,

"Loyalties? To this shyster's paradise? To these potters of twopenny creams for sale at twenty times the price under an assumed name? *Sleek! Nearness!* Why can't you . . ."

"*Sleek*'s very good. I use it."

"Loyalties! And what about our extra half-hours filched from lunch? What about your dentist? I'm your dentist, and my chair's in the Spinning Wheel. I'm the first dentist with a rocking-chair. And I'm your poor old grandmother you buried!" he shouted. "Why you'd cheat them soon as look at them!"[59]

While she tries to make him lower his voice, she vows inwardly to make the most of the day—her last day of freedom. She doesn't credit him with more sense about Allosol than she has. Then he rushes off for injections and promises to call back soon.

XXVII   *The Office Party*

The development of the novel takes place once the Christmas party begins. Sansom draws upon his own experiences at office parties which give workers an opportunity to emerge more as individuals amid a setting of chaos and alcoholic blur. He also draws upon his daily perusal of trade gazettes such as *Fur and Feathers* and *Leather Trades*. From these gazettes he obtained the idea that H.J., the boss, adopts, that of diversifying his business and buying leather goods.[60] Because of this diversification, the Christmas bonuses are small. Therefore the party begins on a sad note. H.J. "courageously" tells everyone personally in the belief that his personal charm will temper disappointment. Like many executives in a position of power, he feels invulnerable to criticism because he has sold himself on his own story of why the bonuses are halved. Sansom understands bosses well in his depiction of H.J.'s lack of concern over his employees' disappointment.

Only one employee dares to voice criticism—Mansford, whose wife is about to give birth to their first child. He does not understand how Allosol can expand and consolidate at the same time. In dialogue that became associated in the 1960s with the theater of the absurd, other employees try to figure out the paradox.

"You consolidate," Mavis sniffed, "*to* expand. Or you expand *to* consolidate—with credit facilities. Surely the great financial brain opposite is aware of this."

"All I'm aware of," Tiny said, popping his eyes right out round from under the long pale lashes, "is wheels within wheels. With special reference to a certain motor-car by Bentley the personal property of an individual to wit Mister Honest Jack. I don't see *that* machine suddenly bereft of half its wheels."[61]

While their attempts at logic evaporate in the injustice of the affair, Mark Deane, the boss's nephew, frowns. He knows that the directors have voted themselves an increase of fees. Both resentment of his special place in the firm and anger over the injustice to the employees rile him. He joins them in drinking ginger wine to forget the pain of bonuses.

Part of the ice-breaking at the party occurs when petty rivalries emerge. Monica compliments Sandra on her brooch, which is an old one, rather than on the new dress that Nevile Wrasse has just bought for her. Sandra flirts with Mark Deane despite his lewd sneer. She also defies Monica, the boss's mistress and head of the typing pool. When she spies a diamond clasp on the rug, fallen from Monica's handbag, she realizes it is a gift from the boss. She hides it for future mischief.

Then Ralph Mansford, salesman and expectant father, pulls Sandra into a storeroom. She thinks, "It was when their wives had babies that they were their wildest, wasn't it? She looked up at him, raising her chin so that he could see the dimple between the tops of her breasts."[62] Immediately after he kisses her, he vomits all over a smashed case of scent, which Sansom humorously dubs *Moujik*. This comic relief, familiar in the romantic scenes of *The Loving Eye* and *The Cautious Heart*, becomes more grotesque and crude than formerly. Perhaps the problem is that the point of view is female here rather than male. Or, Sansom may be conscious of the banality of the scene and may be trying to liven it. Whatever the reason, Ralph, soon after vomiting, learns that his wife has died in childbirth and left him with an infant daughter. This news sets a pall over the party. Dissension breaks out and Monica discovers that her diamond clasp is lost.

Mark proposes a police-type of line-up of all the secretaries in order to find out who stole the diamond clasp. The transistor radio blares, "Here we go gathering NUTS IN MAY!" as everyone joins hands and dances about the room.

Sandra, feeling Monica's pin digging into her, retreats into H.J.'s office to dislodge it. In the silence of his plush office she feels a hollow nothingness. In an effort to confront her real self, she strips off her clothes and hides the diamond pin in the carpet near the desk. Then she hums as she prances about the office nude. This movement gives Sansom an opportunity to pun on Sandra's inner thoughts.

Really, I'm doing it for Bun—it'll be Sarawak or nothing after this first and last appearance! Really—Allasol, to shake the party up, for H.J.'s sake! My good heavens, I'll give 'em nuts in May, I'll put May in their nuts. . . .[63]

She is still fantasizing that she will do something exciting. But when H.J. comes into the office in search of the missing clip and coughs uncomfortably at the sight of her nakedness, her hopes fall. She realizes no one is searching her out for their game of Nuts-in-May. She begins to cry quietly. When she hears her name being called, however, she dresses hastily, leaving her black panties in H.J.'s wastebasket.

Later on, the wise cleaning woman, Mrs. Tovey, assures Sandra that there will be a lot more exciting things in life even if she does marry and live in faraway Sarawak. While Sandra is annoyed at Mrs. Tovey's mundane advice, she is pacified. As people leave the party, she returns to H.J.'s office to retrieve her panties.

As she enters the darkened office, she hears muffled sounds like tears. She discovers H.J. and Monica in the sex act on the old leather sofa. Suddenly Sandra defiantly turns on the light. She is burning with delight and vengeance. H.J. is furious and fires her on the spot. But she rejoins that she is leaving anyway. Then she calls Monica "Pussy," H.J.'s nickname for her and leaves with her black panties, laughing uncontrollably.

XXVIII   *The Weakness of* The Last Hours of Sandra Lee

Sandra's encounters with authority figures and seducers are, for the most part, without surprise. Her naiveté even seems banal. It is obvious from the beginning that she will marry her intended so that her last hours follow the righteous path of romantic fiction from women's magazines. For example, the last line reads: "To where that night she was to 'become a woman,' though this, in every crucial way, she had surely become in the last and full flowering of the ended hour."[64]

The setting of the cosmetic firm also becomes boring after awhile. Sansom seems to have wrung as much irony as possible from the absurd names of products and animism from unlikely objects. Only the false front of the firm to its employees on the subject of halved bonuses succeeds in containing a deeper meaning.

The novel was published in the United States under the title *The Wild Affair*. This is perhaps more deceptive than the original title, *The Last Hours of Sandra Lee*. Sandra is neither wild nor prone to affairs.

On the other hand, the theme of Sandra's search for her true identity is worthwhile. In the end, she returns to her given name of Marjorie and supposedly comes to terms with herself. Sansom is really interested in depicting her life more by aesthetic than by moral standards. The falseness of the cosmetic merchandise emphasizes the aesthetic issues. Sandra-Marjorie is in search of an image of a free, modern girl. But Sansom glosses over why she settles for what she really does not want but is led to believe she wants. Perhaps this is too difficult to depict because of his use of a third-person-female subjective point of view; as in *A Bed of Roses*, the female point of view does not come easily to him.

Michel-Michot finds the greatest danger in Sansom's approach here "is that he believes he can build an interesting novel round an uninteresting person."[65] Obviously he cannot do this. Only his descriptions and authorial comments relieve the novel from the triviality of the characters' conversations and ideas.

XXIX Goodbye

Like *The Last Hours of Sandra Lee*, *Goodbye*, published in 1966, is rooted in the modern world. The protagonist, Anthony Lyle, investment banker, homeowner, husband, and father, reacts to the modern way of life, and in particular to the issues of modern marriage. *Goodbye* presages a phenomenon of the 1970s: the dissolution of marriages of twenty years or more at the demand of the wife. She appears often to have no specific reasons, to wish to be independent of male dominance, and to feel disenchanted with her role after the children have grown up.

Tony Lyle is Mr. Average. In the context of the Welfare State and affluent society, he feels rootless. In preparation for this novel, Sansom has noted that Mr. Average is a man ". . . [whose] conversation may be all clichés, he may be very much of a bore: but feel, beyond words, he does."[66] Sansom's concern is for the individual whom modern man ignores. As in the early story "The Forbidden Lighthouse," he is repelled by the mob who pressure individuals to resist the world of fantasy in favor of a conformist world of sameness. Yet he has no solutions to offer the suffering individual.

XXX *Holograph Notes for* Goodbye

From notes on Woodbine cigarette covers, Sansom constructs some of the problems of the characters. He notes for the wife: "The infantile cycles in intelligent women are in evidence. . . . There is said to be in all women a bitch raring to get out. If a woman doesn't deceive her husband, she deceives herself."[67] These notes seem incorporated into the irrational personality of the wife, Zoë.

He notes the following for the husband.

The extraordinary thing is man and woman live together. Entirely different creatures with chemical attraction. Conflict equals survival. . . . Lincoln said, ". . . to make your own decision in spite of what is usual."

To take exact place of parents increases in middle age. . . . The Dionysian
concept of decay is through the grape and harvest and renewal. . . . One of
the reasons for *staying* quarreling is because people are lonely. Where else
can they go? Stand about and fume? And feel lonely? No . . . back they go.
And because both are courageous or obsessed, they carry on.

Whole question of freedom. People invite their gaolers to live with them.
But because they invite, they are their own gaolers. Dichotomy: loneliness or
company in prison.[68]

Thus, Sansom ponders the theme of *Goodbye*. Tony's problems
increase and torment him as the illusion of a secure marriage departs.
He fights acknowledging the truth of his relationship and in the
course of doing so arrives at a bizarre solution of justice.

XXXI   *A Comparison of* The Body *with* Goodbye

Both Henry Bishop and Tony Lyle refuse to face the reality of the
situations that confront them. Henry refuses to supply alternate
interpretations of the actions of Charley Diver and his wife, Madge,
while Tony refuses to understand his wife, Zoë's, changing needs.
Both men tend to sit back and contemplate their homes and gardens,
their achievements as men of property. They also regard their wives
as property. They ignore the quality of life that is changing around
them which is dependent on elements totally out of their control. In
both novels Sansom condemns the absurd conditions in each man's
life which he willingly embraces as security. Settling for a perfunctory
approach to life and doing one's duty are not his definition of
happiness.

Both Henry and Tony are pathetically old-fashioned. They are out
of step with the modern world; thus, they are unable to communicate.
The problem of loneliness is one of the major problems depicted in
contemporary literature. But Henry's loneliness in 1949 seems
remediable while Tony's loneliness in 1966 seems doomed. Perhaps
the difference in views is due to Sansom's own aging process; perhaps
the difference lies in Sansom as a short-story writer and Sansom as a
novelist. As the former, he usually grants his characters the
existential freedom of choice beyond the limits of his own plotting
imagination. As the latter, he is more restrained by the longer length
and the necessity to plot minutely his characters' fate.

In the beginning of the novel, when Tony hears his wife packing
suitcases, he ascribes her action to a row they have had. As he
innocently reviews the row, he cannot understand why his remark

that her friend Sarah Leamington looked "empty" was so incendiary. From Zoë's defense of her friend, the reader gathers that Sarah is an adventurous woman who went to South Africa and returned with strong social and political views against apartheid. In other words, Sarah is a modern woman with curiosity about the changing world. She is not content to be just Mrs. Average Affluent Housewife.

Tony is frightened not only by woman's changing role but also by modern life. He can only resort to his past knowledge of marriage and the clichés about it. He recalls that Zoë has threatened to leave him two or three times before in their eighteen years of marriage. He girds himself for hours of arguing until he can calm her down enough to unpack. He never doubts at the beginning that he will succeed.

But, to his surprise, she calmly continues packing and in the next few days, cooks meals, entertains friends, and indicates plans for a future life doing something meaningful.

Tony attempts to share his despair with several males. First, he tells a neighbor, George Chalcott-Bentinck, who is washing his car in the usual Saturday afternoon ritual. Tony has a limp which he empha-sizes as he approaches George in order to gain sympathy. George is willing to listen to the details of the argument between him and Zoë; however, when Tony says, "Turned me into a woman while she was at it,"[69] George stops the conversation. He is evidently frightened by Tony's confession that he is not taking the separation like a man, which would be to suffer in silence or win the argument by brute tactics.

Next, Tony visits his friend Savory, a bachelor. Together they try to figure out if Zoë is experiencing The Change, a lover, or disenchantment because Tony hasn't brought her flowers from time to time. This is a humorous scene. Tony can only recall Zoë's past behavior, which offers no guidelines for understanding her present behavior.

How can you define a fairly normal soul? Only by exaggeration. Pick on her obsessions? Pick on her periodic outbursts to change the house round, make the dining-room the sitting-room? But you must place against this the long months of quiet. Pounce on the fact that she worked once a year wrapping parcels for the undernourished? Deduce from this a fundamental guilt: tie it in cleverly with that avid scrabbling at nail varnish? With the adulteration of clocks—keeping them five minutes fast to save last-minute rushes—and with the watering of drinks? No, no. It gets out of balance. You are more truly faced with a variable human being, made up of capacities rather than characteristics, and even these are slowly changing all the time.[70]

He does not realize that the habit of living together does not necessarily bring with it closeness. He views marriage with the same bourgeois satisfaction as with things achieved. He also does not realize that accusing Zoë of being theatrical is further evidence of his lack of empathy.

He resorts to a little routine to divert himself. He takes a drink and then walks the dog. He meets a neighbor, Powsey, who gives him a running commentary on the ironies of the Welfare State and the new liberating talk about sex. Tony welcomes an opportunity to talk about the battle of the sexes. But he is horrified by Powsey's loose attitude toward adultery. Powsey admits that both he and his wife have lovers and are enjoying themselves in their middle age. He boasts about his wife's liberation.

"We took a decko at married life biologically rather than sociologically-like. She had to confess to unexpressed yearnings: after, say, a chance eye-up with some good-looking chap in a bus or shop. 'You're inhibited,' I said. She said, 'But we're *married!*' 'Look at it more clinically,' I said. 'What you've got's no more nor less than a social tabu: and there's all your healthy animal instincts withering. You'll get cancer.'"[71]

When Tony asks his boss, Mr. Varley, for leave because of a serious domestic upset, Mr. Varley gives him an avuncular lecture on the strains of middle age that one must adjust to. He assumes Tony is contemplating leaving his wife and angers Tony with a fatuous analogy of marriage to eggs.

"You've been having eggs to your tea, off and on, for just too many years. You're not tired of eggs. You haven't lost your appetite. You *like* eggs. What you've lost is simply the ability to get *excited* about eggs. And that's where the wife comes in. . . . She'll be *there*, with the egg. You'll feel—how shall I say?—more settled about that egg in her company. No need to get excited. *She'll* be there. The substantiation of time, that's her. Your rejection of the egg and its fly-by-night excitement won't hurt so much . . . *don't* cut away. You're going to need her. Don't think you can run off and get the better of time!"[72]

Sansom is obviously enjoying this rhetorical speech. He enjoys the mouthings of pompous people and, consistent with some of his previous humor, trivializing marriage or rather trivializing the sexual aspects of marriage. In Varley's words, sex is an edible staple of life, as depersonalized as an egg but nourishing.

Since it is Zoë who is leaving and not Tony, Varley's warnings are inappropriate. So next Tony turns to a friend, Jack Buckett. Through his wife, Jill, Jack knows of Zoë's intention to leave. But he does not know the reason. Something in Jack's manner of responding to him seems strange to Tony. He later learns that Jack has decided to leave Jill and claims that Tony's situation was the cause. Tony concludes that if his happiness is that catching, he had better wear a leper-bell.

When Jenks, the carpenter, comes to call about building a shed, he offers Tony his sympathy over the news that his wife is leaving. Tony is upset to realize that he had been the subject of the bush telegraph with everyone whispering about him and Zoë.

Finally, he ends up in a strange bar, confiding in an elderly man who looks like a big stiff mullet. The "mullet" tells him that his wife died a year ago and now he has a cat as a companion. This triggers in Tony the fantasy of Zoë dead.

He returns home, slashes Zoë's dress, and vandalizes her room. He reads a letter from their son who is in the navy and can be of no help to him. From this point on, dramatic changes occur. All his friends whom he sought solace from are in turmoil. Powsey's wife leaves him, Savory decides to get married, Jack leaves his wife, and Tony reads in a newspaper a limerick that mocks his car-washing neighbor, Chalcott-Bentinck.

XXXII   *Zoë*

Zoë Lyle is perhaps the only woman in Sansom's novels who is successfully depicted. She does not talk the baby talk of Madge in *The Body*, she does not lie compulsively as Eve does in *The Face of Innocence*, she does not find herself drawn to sadistic, abusive men as Louise in *A Bed of Roses*, she does not pose as Lily in *The Loving Eye*, she does not appear in a sweet blur as Marie in *The Cautious Heart*, and she does not delude herself as Sandra Lee does in *The Last Hours of Sandra Lee*.

Zoë appears as a woman able to assess herself accurately and act courageously when she discovers that her marriage has staled. Unskilled but intelligent, she is willing to take her chances on creating a new life for herself. She has no dreams of magically finding a man or marvelous job but she has plans for survival independent of her husband. She also feels no guilt toward her son, who is now independent and living by himself.

She has considered all kinds of alternatives to the dulled state of marriage. In discussing suicide with Tony and the Bucketts, she says, ". . . The most curious and not unusual reason for suicide seems to be happiness . . . or what we search for in the name of happiness."[73] She is individualistic enough not to be influenced by what others consider happiness. But Tony fails to pick up her reason for leaving. He is stubbornly obtuse about recognizing her disenchantment with marriage. Try as he may to analyze her daily life, he cannot find what is missing. Cleaning house, shopping, meeting people and talking with them, seeing a film or exhibition do not seem *that* boring to him.

When she is busy in the kitchen, Tony assumes she has relented and the whole affair will evaporate. Even when he makes love to her, he expects a reconciliation. But Zoë's dispassionate embrace and impersonal words anger him. When he reproaches her for letting him make love to her, she tells him that she likes it. This response makes him feel empty and, in typical Sansomian cynicism, he labels marriage as nothing more than legalized prostitution.

Ironically, for all his indignation, he visits a prostitute a few days later. With her, he does not smart under feelings of being exploited whereas with Zoë he views himself as the exploited and abused one.

Finding Zoë all dressed up and made up, ready to go on a shopping trip, he asks if she is meeting a man. She denies it. Then he asks if she can afford a shopping trip. She laughs and says it will be her last time in London for awhile. She also gives a significant answer to his question of whether she has saved enough money for a shopping spree: "Certainly. Part of the payment for some of the best years of my life. But not all of them. There lies the point. Now I really must dash."[74]

When Tony comments aloud on the dangers of having a woman judge who is menopausal, Zoë flares up "with a fearful comparison of a lonely old male judiciary full of port and the bellyache, prostate trouble and wig-itch."[75]

Tony seems incapable of avoiding delicate subjects, which makes the reader suspect that through the years it has been Zoë who has accepted his gaucherie with patience. If so, it is no wonder that she has decided to leave him. He treats her like a male friend in a bar-room, adumbrating her with every stale male cliché about women. He bumbles,

Sex was an elevated eating . . . and like other organic functions sieved through the human brain it had many forms—just like everything else . . . so you could have farmyard sex or gourmet's sex or troubadour's non-sex, or prisoner's hunger-bread sex, or curiosity-killed-the-keyhole sex, or climb-Everest-sex and so on. . . . "Yes," she said vaguely, "like anything else there's lots of kinds of it. But a woman likes to lose herself," she said. "Farmyard?" he asked. "Celestially," she breathed. "Cow-shmow," he smiled, "celestial-bestial." She shut up.[76]

Obviously Zoë is more cerebral than Tony and more sensitive to others. His conversion of sex to food and acts of prurience typifies his crudeness. The unfortunate thing is his unawareness of just how crude he is. His bantering reveals his own puritan attitude toward sex; he isolates it as a dirty but necessary part of marriage.

Until Tony slashes her clothes, which is the turning point of the story, Zoë is evasive. But when he deals with his self-pity by vandalizing her room, she finally confesses her reasons for leaving.

". . . I stupidly thought I could manage this without hurting you too much. And I stupidly hung about here instead of getting clear away, as I see I should have done.

"You ask your big Why. Well—phrases like 'I've fallen out of love with you' hardly suit our time of life. The truth is I've fallen out of any interest in you whatsoever.

"To me, you're nothing, absolutely nothing.

"I don't hate you, I don't even dislike you. I just don't feel anything about you. And who in God's reasonable name wants to go on living side by side with a nothing? It's no company. . . .

"It takes you to make me lonely. When I'm alone, I'm not lonely. But when you're about the house there still seems to be some slight and messy thread which spoils the solitude one might expect if you were really nothing, just air."[77]

Her words accurately describe the apathy she feels which is opposite to love/hate. She is very much a person of the present. Unlike Tony, she does not need the security of the past traditions in order to handle her feelings of self-esteem. She is willing to take risks.

In his stunned state, Tony is kissed by Mange, the dog. He sees a huge bottle of Zoë's sleeping pills on her trunk. These pills set into motion his revenge for her abandonment of him.

XXXIII   *The Pessimism of* Goodbye

The suicide note that Tony prepares for both Zoë and himself is as boring as Tony has become to the reader. Once he is certain that Zoë will leave him, he decides the only solution is to kill her through an overdose of pills in her drink and also to kill himself the same way. Sansom seems to be pessimistic about middle-aged men's chances for creating a new life. He does not seem to be pessimistic about a middle-aged woman's chances, however. But he implies that the Lyles only felt happy while overcoming the difficulties of establishing a home, family, and career. Middle age, instead of giving them a new lease on life, has become as bland and secure as the welfare state. There seems to be nothing to worry about, nothing to achieve, and no more reason for husbands and wives to pull together.

Even the minor characters echo Sansom's pessimism. Each one is embroiled in a lusterless marriage or relationship; each one feels numb about his sense of loneliness.

With Tony's typical insensitivity toward Zoë, he prepares two strong poisonous drinks. Since she does not like strong drinks, she substitutes a weaker one for herself. Tony does not know this. He goes ahead and drinks the poisoned drink and dies, never having achieved the revenge on Zoë that he craved.

Tony cannot even stage a successful murder-suicide. Like the cab driver in Chekhov's "Lament," who is so alienated from people that he can only confide his troubles in his horse, Tony can only confide his to his dog, Mange.

A reviewer in the *New Statesman* says of this novel,

... [Sansom] doesn't give his characters a chance; they're not so much naturally as artificially inadequate—no more than good sport for baiting. And this isn't only unpleasant, it gives the novel an air of contrivance. The would-be tragedy at the end is thrown away. It isn't the hero's fault that he pathetically traps himself into suicide. It was the author who saw to that.[78]

The reviewer feels that Tony's lack of imagination and sensitivity to anyone else vitiates the strong depiction of Zoë and her contemporary problem as a middle-aged housewife. To be a challenge to a wife like this, Tony should have more range of feelings other than pride and revenge.

Another reviewer, in the *Times Literary Supplement*, says,

... His effects are obtained by revealing a state of mind through dialogue and descriptions exaggerated and made slightly fantastic. There are passages in this book which are as good as anything he has done.... At the end ... however, one is left asking whether these impressive parts form any kind of meaningful whole. Lyle never seems remotely like a foreign bond and exchange dealer, or anything but a totally artificial creation. Zoë's own character is a blank . . . the people most vividly seen here as in much of Mr. Sansom's work, are the minor figures fixed by a single characteristic, rather like a Jonsonian humor. Much of *Goodbye* is interesting and amusing, but it is a succession of Catherine wheels rather than a coherent fireworks show.[79]

Discouraged by these reviews and similar ones, Sansom left the issues of the welfare state and middle age in the novel form behind him. He also did not write another novel for five years. Instead he wrote short stories, collections of travel stories, and essays.

XXXIV   Hans Feet in Love

The idea for a picaresque novel about a buffoon named Hans Feet occurs quite early in Sansom's papers. But he did not write *Hans Feet in Love* until the late 1960s. It was published in 1971 to what became the worst notices any books of his have ever received.

Hans Feet in Love is really a number of short stories about the amorous successes and plentiful failures of a prurient salesman. He slowly learns the truth about the illusion of a footloose, bachelor existence—that chasing women can also be a lonely, meaningless existence.

Hans Feet appears to be a caricature based on Sansom's own childhood fears. He has talked about them as follows:

As a child, I had always been shy and self-conscious. Then at 17 I lost control of my voice. For about three years I could either shout or speak in a whisper. . . . This embarrassment was complicated by a fairly fictitious fear of a poor physique—narrow-chested, buck-toothed. . . . Even today with these qualms somewhat settled, disguised by beard and ebonpoint, I feel more like a bag of artificial gestures moving about than a body. The upshot was that I spent years, awful years, from 17 to about 23, as a proper young paranoiac.[80]

Hans Feet is a composite of these fictitious fears. He is lacking in self-confidence, particularly about his name. "At his first school, the little boys and girls had danced round him cruelly singing: 'Hands, Feet and Boompsi-daisy.' At his later school, the more sophisticated older boys labelled him Hans Foetus. . . . [As he matures he becomes] an almost professional second-rater. Second, never first in class. Second, never first in races, in teams."[81] He becomes sexually aroused easily but is not successful with his first woman. This produces a sadness in him that opens his eyes to the beauty of the world. His first successful sale of encyclopedias, however, gives him hope for a new life as an adult.

Against the background of an increasingly permissive society, Hans finds that not all women are so permissive when it comes to his gauche advances. He has many encounters: with a girl in a graveyard, a woman with a passion for crayfish, a lady in love with a cricket umpire, a Lebanese painter with curious ideas about his role, and many other women who are full of surprises for him.

At the end of his adventures he meets a woman who appears to be a mouse but is actually Rita Brown, an articulate, energetic woman. Why she returns his affection remains a mystery, but, in typical romantic fashion, she becomes Rita Feet.

While Hans reveals the same irresistible urge of many Sansom males to inquire about Rita's previous lovers and to lament jealously that they existed, he still finds happiness. He works as a salesman who heads a sales-school (which is Sansom's gentle poke at the Peter Principle)— and, in his leisure moments, he carves stone angels, Bibles, and floral crosses. Sansom wrings as much comedy out of this sentimental conformist's life as possible. He says,

But, of course, life was not all angels and hot cakes. . . . They had their private jokes. One of these, very naturally, was that name of theirs. . . . Early on, he had applauded her for the brave front she had put on to the jingle of Rita Feet. And afterwards, they had begun a series of jokes about the names of their children to come. It was difficult to find a safe one. Peter Feet rhymed, Deirdre Feet became dirty feet. Others, like Polly and Anna, sounded like plastic materials and patent medicines, polyphere and anafete. Oliver Feet was all-over feet, and Denise Feet no more than a physical jerk.[82]

Having wrung all the puns possible out of Hans's name, Sansom concludes the novel with a modern allusion: Hans experiences an annunciation in the form of a smile on the face of one of the angels he is carving out of stone. This evokes the suspicion that perhaps marriage is not all there is to life. He decides to breed in order to continue his line. The novel ends with Hans urging Rita to throw away the Pill.

The reviewers excoriated Sansom for this novel. James Hughes, in a review entitled "Losing Hans Down in the Sex Stakes," called it

. . . a real bummer. . . . Casual sex may be more available now than it was when Mr. Sansom was a boy, but the actual technique of chatting up birds is probably no easier to master than it ever was. The archaic vocabulary and the agonized facetiousness of the style accurately reflect the sort of chatter you can hear at any party where nervous, single men are trying to make out.[83]

Another reviewer called it a "flat-footed" novel.
Sansom himself said of it years later,

> . . . [My] subconscious impulses . . . are perhaps the most intriguing mystery of all. . . . I have been astonished to find suspicious cases of it in . . . for instance . . . *Hans Feet in Love*, which turns out to be full of teeth and dogs with teeth which I never consciously intended. Unknown to me, did I deeply want to bite the central character into more determined action, wake him up? Or did I want him to be eaten up? I shall never know.[84]

Nor shall the reader ever know. One may speculate that Sansom, having made notes for this novel ten years before, was trying to salvage an enticing idea. Perhaps he felt that the more openly sexual aspects of society would provide receptivity to Hans and his pratfalls. Or, middle age might have been palling so that he thought he would enliven the public by recollections of a young man's folly. Whatever the reason, *Hans Feet in Love* is far below Sansom's usual high standards of novel-writing.

XXXV   A Young Wife's Tale

A Young Wife's Tale, published in 1974, is Sansom's last novel. While it is a vast improvement over its predecessor, *Hans Feet in Love*, it is not without some problems.

The plot seems improbable. An Italian contessa forces a young electronic-music composer apart from his wife for a year, ostensibly to further his career. The young wife returns to London and loneliness. She falls prey to two men, but surprisingly, at the same time, becomes a successful artist. Within the year the couple are together again, but they have to pay a price for the contessa's obdurate demands.

Sansom claims the idea for the novel came from several sources. First, he had been vacationing in Tuscany and he felt there was a background there that had not yet been treated in fiction. Second, he recalled a story, "In Love," by Alfred Hays, which he had read thirty years before. It was about a happy wife and husband who go to a nightclub. Alone at a nearby table is a handsome man, five years older than the wife. While the husband is busy, the stranger asks the wife for a dance. During the dance, he proposes to pay her an enormous amount of money if she will spend one night in bed with him. She accepts. Sansom did not recall the ending and did not look it up. Instead, he rewrote the story in more ordinary terms. The English wife turns a blind eye on the machinations of the contessa with her husband. She becomes so successful at painting that she doesn't need the materialism the contessa offers. Third, Sansom used his knowledge of the lavish entertainment enjoyed abroad by businessmen with grave risks to their marriage relationships.[85]

XXXVI   *Julie as Narrator*

Julie, the young wife, tells the story from the first-person point of view. With all the muted anger of a Jean Rhys character, Julie endlessly obsesses about the malevolence of the Contessa Renata, whom she nicknames The Nose. Her first impression of the contessa in the Tuscan village of Santa Vilga notes a snake-face, eyes "like grey jade, a very beautiful snake: with a very, very long nose, a rigidly poised snake in itself. . . . I fell in hate at first sight."[86] She fears her power and aggressiveness when she finds out that the contessa is interested in her husband's electronic beep-music. And she is, of course, correct. The contessa does exact a hard bargain with Mark: he is to work with her on music for a film while she promotes him as a new talent, but he is to live apart from Julie for a year or two in order to devote himself totally to his work.

Kay Dick, in a review of the novel in the *Scotsman*, finds Julie's confessions "not quite credible, in the sense that as she is drawn to appear intelligent her gushing femininities about her husband's body and behaviour belong not quite to our age."[87]

For example, Julie says,

Mark is six foot and about an inch, grizzled blondish hair, small eyes with a secret twinkle, heavenly long serious jowls. I love these jowls. Doggy, my man. A right tall hound of a husband. And full of beeps. A devout composer of electronic music, he must be full of secret beeps. That "Well, well" was like a kind of beeping. He doesn't say much. How could he, with all that going on inside him?"[88]

In her eyes he is always the innocent boy being led astray by the sophisticated contessa. Nevertheless, Julie does reveal sensitivity to

Mark's personality in her understanding of his background prior to her meeting him.

> ... Apart from the arms he used somehow to fling over the back of a chair, as if he were his own coathanger, and apart from those loose-crossed legs with their little socks showing white bits of calf like an abbreviated male can-can dancer, apart from so many other physical facets, like his irritating little sniff through one nostril to denote concentration and like the beautiful pock-marks of long-past boyhood boils on the back of his lovely neck, apart from all this I had a dossier: age, thirty-three, son of a middling prosperous chandler. Plymouth born and London raised. School for the Sons of Gentlemen and University for All, modern studies. After a year in France, entered British rat-race as advertising consultant. Now had to semi-maintain wife. No children. Which could of course run otherwise: age thirty-three, lonely childhood concerned with himself, aptitude for games, masturbation in speechless France, dreams of girls and poetry one day turning into beeps because of record heard on one-day trip to Holland.[89]

Here Julie reveals perception that she often does not reveal elsewhere. Although she is aware that Mark's head is full of beeps, she still tries to impugn Mark's relationship with the contessa.

Even when Julie confronts the elegant contessa with the unacceptable conditions of the deal, she fails to sustain the argument. She becomes self-conscious of her own unkempt looks and feels deflated. Considering the comfortable middle-class background that Sansom gives Julie and her ownership of an antique shop that is prospering, her cowed reaction before the contessa's elegance seems highly unlikely. Sansom appears to make too much fuss over the contessa's money and title. It is questionable whether a young woman of the 1970s would fuss over them as much. Furthermore, Sansom allows only one epithet for the contessa, "The Nose," to blemish her. And it is used so much that it becomes tedious.

When Julie finally accepts her husband's venture and he has gone off with the contessa to start publicity work, Julie begins to rethink her position. She has been asked to cooperate by returning home to England. Although they will write to each other, she must not try to see her husband. Julie interprets this as a request to let her husband bed down the contessa and for Julie to stay on ice for a long time. Feeling like a woman whose actor-husband has been given a chance to tour Hollywood for publicity's sake, she tries to live alone in London. But after a few months her love and trust of Mark ebb and she feigns illness in order to get him home. When a friend of Mark, a homosexual, comes to visit and iron his clothes, he leaves some in her flat. Soon after Mark pays a flying visit to London and returns to the flat while Julie is out. Finding men's underwear there, he leaves her an angry note.

While they straighten out the misunderstanding by slow mail and unanswered phone calls, Julie has an adventure with a man she meets in a bar who turns out to be impotent. So she is saved from infidelity by a technicality.

XXXVII   *Setting and Description*

The Tuscan landscape is given full tribute by Sansom's descriptive powers. From a hill overlooking the village, Julie describes the view.

Our eminence enlarged it, you could now only see the edge of town, with a wide seascape and sequences of bays and promontories stretched far off to a greying distance. The sea was like a vast bowl of greenish milk of almonds, outrageously calm and pure; this was the moment before sunset, when breezes dropped before beginning their nightly offshore stint. A moment of pause, of a beauty that successfully ached.[90]

Not only the visual senses are indulged but also the auditory because of Mark's sensitive ears and his omnipresent tape-recorder. He records the burring of cicadas, the roar of the Mediterranean waves, the squelch of naked heels on ice-cream cartons lying on the beach, and other "beeping" and "glupping."

The project Renata contracts Mark for is a science-fiction film in which some phenomenon "turned machines into flesh, not as is usual the other way around, but about, say, animated typewriters full of their own blood, about love affairs of hoovers, the giant copulations of power stations. . . ."[91] Sansom's comic touches are effective in his calling these sound effects flesh music or a new dimension of "pornophony."

After Mark has left with the contessa, Julie is alone in Santa Vilga. Sansom is at his best describing the effect of nature on her emotions.

It was the hottest time of day, the heat was vast. Yet none of the garish plants about drooped, they stood there in their tropical-looking spikes and curves in absolute green and yellow vigour, carved. The coloured flowers hissed brilliance. They seemed to be forcing themselves under a glass of heat. And yet were slyly moving—from one or two bushes heavy seeds dropped. They dropped with the absolute plop of a ball. At long irregular intervals. . . . Soon it became a hammer glow. A ticking clock can be bad: this was worse, it was a kind of water torture in pure sound, you waited in silence, the suspense ballooned, it would never come, the whole air and everything and time expanded to breaking point which did not break—and then it did, plop, a release and a heavy blow at once, and then the whole thing, the silence, the expanse, the blow began again.[92]

The beautiful resort now becomes like a cell and she resembles a prisoner suffering water torture. Her anxieties smother her in much the same way that the vast heat of the day does. As this atmosphere thickens, she takes action. Before leaving, she performs a slight act of revenge. While diving underwater and collecting specimens, she comes upon the anchor of the *Spada*, Renata's yacht. She knows Renata and Mark are away in Germany, but she also knows that in the future the yacht will carry them places to film and gain publicity. The *Spada* stands for the power that great wealth has which she feels powerless to fight. She swims against the anchor line of the yacht and lashes it. The line floats away and with it the cloud of the yacht above her. When she surfaces, she shouts that the boat is being smashed against the rocks on one side. She is so triumphant that she does not even feel relief than no one on board was harmed.

XXXVIII *Reversals and Surprises*

Sansom has given a reverse twist to almost every complication in the novel. Julie finally commits adultery with a farmer and conceives a child. She becomes equally as famous as Mark for her creativity—painting. The contessa turns out to be a lesbian—she had never had sexual designs on Mark.

Sansom ends with a moral in the words of Julie:

Perhaps it's my fault, for the feeling that I've been trustless and untrustworthy erodes, and the more deeply because it had been unfairly diverted against him. Perhaps it's Mark's fault, perhaps his natural remoteness grows too much for me to take: his consuming fidelity to his work, my passing infidelity to him—which makes for the deeper rift? Or perhaps it is all far more simple, simply a change in our fortunes, no longer the small struggle of two-together against a hard-looking world?[93]

This moralistic tone contains shades of the early fireman stories. While the separation of the couple raises ambiguities, it appears to be a metaphor for the inevitable separateness that exists in marriage. Even though the situation that thrusts the couple into jeopardy is contrived, the doubts and struggles of Julie contain verisimilitude. Also, Sansom chooses not to write a frothy happy ending as he did in two previous novels. He attempts to break that formula with a jarring note at the end.

XXXIX *Critical Reactions to* A Young Wife's Tale

While most critics called *A Young Wife's Tale* light fiction, they praised Sansom's style, wit, and deftness in describing the Tuscan setting.

Valentin Cunningham in the *New Stateman* says,

Sansom is fetchingly jokey (a couple of painted ladies are instantly dubbed World Whore One and Two: wish *I'd* thought of that), but he does have this annoying trick of laying claim to more out-of-the-way experiences than this reader, certainly, can truthfully boast: "If you've ever made love outside in the hot summer rain, say in a thunderstorm, you will know what I mean."[94]

On the other hand, Anthony Thwaite, in the *Observer*, criticizes Sansom for his rococo style of never letting anything pass without an adornment. He terms *A Young Wife's Tale* a "souffle" that must rise in a frothy peak and not collapse into tasteless realism. He writes of a recent trip to Prague in which he discovered that Sansom was one of the few contemporary British writers in translation.

. . . It occurs to me . . . that this may be because there's something convincingly decadent about his work. The decline of the capitalist West is froth and frills and trivia. I don't want to turn heavy about this, because Mr. Sansom is a deft entertainer; but I do find a bit depressing the thought that the city of Kafka (who represents a less winsome form of decadence) may take the mannered frivolities of Sansom as representative of current British fiction.[95]

Whether Thwaite is ruling out entertainment in the novel is unclear. Certainly the romantic fiction of Sansom's later novels is a far cry from social realism. But they fill a need and supply the reader with a polished prose style.

Other critics felt that the choice of a woman as narrator is the main problem. As in *The Last Hours of Sandra Lee*, Sansom is unsuccessful with the woman's point of view. His novels told from the man's point of view are much more believable.

On the other hand, Julie, like Zoë in *Goodbye*, represents Sansom's growing mastery of delving into the mind of an intelligent,

sensitive woman. The main problem in understanding Julie's morality and inhibitions exists in the distance of Sansom's generation from
hers. Julie seems tormented by the moral dilemmas of a much older
woman, say, someone who matured in the 1930s rather than the
1960s. In the sexually uninhibited 1970s it is questionable whether
Julie would have agonized so much over committing adultery as
revenge for the adultery she fantasies Mark is committing. And, it is
not even questionable whether readers would accept this agonizing as
realistic. They would not!

XL   *Summary of the Novels*

In the twenty-five year period during which Sansom wrote his nine
novels, several changes in his work took place. He joined the majority
of writers in Britain who wrote novels in the tradition of realism. At
the same time, he wrote short stories that did not hew to the realistic
tradition.

If the twenty-five years are divided roughly into thirds, the first
third contains his best novels: *The Body*, *The Loving Eye*, and *The
Cautious Heart*. These novels share the strength of a male point of
view either first person or third person, a protagonist obsessed by a
problem relating to a woman, and a setting that is well-integrated
with the action of the story. These novels achieve a delicate play of
illusion and reality as the complexities of the characters are revealed.
By the time he wrote *The Loving Eye*, Sansom's comic sense was also
emerging.

In the second third, Sansom turned away from obsessed characters
and toward the effect of the post-war environment on ordinary
people. Whenever he wrote from the female point of view, he
produced a weaker work. When he returned to the male point of view,
as in *Goodbye*, he succeeded in writing a stronger work. His own
growing middle-age with its absorption in past manners and morals
appears more dominant in the novels of this period. But he also
appears to be creating more convincing women characters; they are
no longer stereotypes. His descriptive powers are as eloquent as ever;
however, the subjects he chooses to describe, such as a cosmetic firm
or suburban neighborhoods, are not always of interest. Perhaps the
greatest problem of this period is his choice of dull protagonists with
whom the reader can neither identify nor laugh.

The last third of his novel-writing career featured sophomoric or
old-fashioned characters, such as Hans and Julie, who are supposed

to be young adults but sound like middle-aged sentimentalists. The humor in these novels is often contrived. But the setting always ennobles the tone so that what emerges from these romantic comedies is Sansom's superb control of plot by his descriptive powers rather than by his powers of depicting character.

In summary, Sansom's interest in the novel form remained fixed but he shifted his emphasis from interesting characters to dull ones, from serious fiction to light, romantic fiction, and from exploration of the inner man to the effects of contemporary life on the outer man.

CHAPTER 4

Books Related to Travel

FOR many years, Sansom was commissioned by magazines, such as *Holiday*, to write about different countries. With his knowledge of several languages, he traveled all over Europe. From these travels, he wrote essays and developed a new form of short-story writing based on various areas and their mores.

The travel essays appear in the following collections: *Pleasure Strange and Simple* (1953); *The Icicle and the Sun* (1958); *Blue Skies, Brown Studies* (1961); *Away to It All* (1964); and *Grand Tour Today* (1968). While these essays reveal Sansom's talent for unusual and typical details, they are commercial writings aimed at the tourist.

On the other hand, the travel–short stories are finely crafted. Outgrowths of travel assignments, they creatively blend exotic locales with a story. Sansom called them "hybrid things in which I graft fiction onto true things against a background of known places."[1] These stories also provide an important link between the early Kafkaesque or Poe-like short stories and the later stories which touched on a wide variety of themes. Three collections of this genre exist: *South* (1948); *The Passionate North* (1950); and *A Touch of Sun* (1952).

I South

The stories in *South* have a quality of anything-can-happen-here, *here* being Greece, Italy, and southern France. To Sansom's highly cerebral characters, these countries hide their primitivism behind a delicate, ornamental facade. Sansom's descriptions of these facades are worthy of the best writing of Proust, about whom he later wrote a book, *Proust and His World*.

"Tutti-Frutti" is a story about a Swede, Ohlsson, a fatalist who visits Nice in November. As he walks about the Place Massena in search of romance, he finds in arcades

97

ceilings [that] still revealed a faded painting of roses and ribbons, of putti and florid friezes, of mandolins and exotic fruits; and . . . pillars beneath painted corinthian capitals still showed a leprous residue of curled lettering advertising from another century: "Chocolat Klaus"; "Banque des Valeurs Metallurgiques"; "Le Parfum de la Vraie Violette"; and even a performance at the Opera dated some seventy years before. Everywhere hung the faded fragrance of expensive years that had offered all the fruits—the chocolate-box years. Years of parasol and cylindre, of Verdi and Berlioz and Paganini, of patchouli and the attars.[2]

As if on cue, a beautiful woman appears. So does a horse-drawn carriage out of the last century. Both the woman and Ohlsson hail the cab. Then a chocolate-box romance ensues as they spend the day together touring Nice.

A sad ending, straight from a Verdi opera, occurs that evening. Ohlsson returns to his hotel to dress for dinner with the woman. He lights a cigarette and leans forward at the window of his hotel room to inhale the night. As he drops his cigarette on the crowd below, he reaches out to retrieve it. He loses his balance and falls four stories. He does not die; he becomes paralyzed for life. The woman never knows why he does not appear at her hotel because he does not wish to inflict on her the bathos of his predicament which will confirm her strong belief in fatalism.

Another sad tale in *South* is "Three Dogs of Siena." It is told from the point of view of an unknown narrator who observes the entrance into Siena of three dogs, Enrico, Osvaldo, and Fa. The story begins: "The Italians love their dogs. And their dogs love the Italians—it is probably to show something of this love that these dogs take such care to reproduce themselves, not in the dull matrix of formal breed, but in most brilliant assortment, in a profusion of wild and unpredictable shape. . . ." The narrator hypothesizes what the dogs see, smell and hear. This is the kind of fantasizing that Sansom does best:

. . . Frowning behind his forward hair, Enrico must have remembered the alleys of Naples, redolent of life and all odour. Osvaldo's fox-like ears would have trembled to the unheard echo of the bustling Genoese arcades. Small Fa's great tail fanned blindly for the warm resistance of all those exudations that thickened the air above the green canal by which once he had lived.[4]

The three friends romp about, enjoying the week of festivities and crowds. Finally, the last day a group of marchers with flags perform a

Sbandierata, a flourish of flags toward their votive church. The three dogs are terrified at the swooping and tossing of flags. As one, they race toward a huge flag that is circling low to the ground—and meet their fate. As they tear at the swathe of the flag, their faces get lashed. The ceremony does not stop for them. The standard-bearers are busy with their flags. The dogs continue to yelp until they are kicked out of the way, half-dead. Sansom concludes with an ironic twist to his opening lines:

> The Italians love their dogs as they love life—but they also love ceremony, and in all ceremony there is the touch of death. The will to live may also be the will to die. Whether it is a rite of harvest or marriage or church, death resides somewhere in the pomp, the order, the finality—and what is always a sense of immolation.[5]

Here Sansom has captured the religious ceremony of Siena with relentless fervor. Also, he subtly contrasts the Italian indifference to cruelty to animals with the English horror of it.

II   The Passionate North

The stories in *The Passionate North* are set in northern Europe. Kay Dick comments on the diction in these stories: ". . . [Sansom is] known as the expert excavator of the unusual—the unusual words, the unusual situations, the unusual landscape, the unusual sensation, the unusual use of the unusual."[6]

Sansom balances landscape with event. More important than this is his confiding in the reader about himself as both a writer and a man. The opening paragraph of "A World of Glass" provides important information about his attitudes toward writing as a profession.

> Cells become writers. Writers are solitaries and cells are solitary: here I can sit in imposed solitude, free from my pity of solitude self-imposed, absolved from all decision and responsibility and all question of selecting diversions of the outside world. Physically I can choose practically nothing: mentally I am freer than before. I must simply sit here and serve my sentence. It was, of course, for assault.[7]

He is speaking in the persona of an Englishman visiting Trondhjem, Norway. He has assaulted another Englishman and is imprisoned. From his cell he tells his story and also tells the reader about Sansom, the solitary man who lives chiefly by observing other peoples' lives.

The story flashes back to the narrator's visit in the quaint white northern town. He meets at the quay a beautiful young native woman. She speaks lovingly of the scenic splendors of the town. The narrator, as is typical in these stories, quickly builds in his mind a fantasy about the unknown woman. He is disappointed to hear that she is married, but his hopes rise when she confesses that, since he is leaving the next day, she does not love her husband.

Then she changes the subject to admiration of the view. She says, "I used to think the station looked like a palace out there with sun gold along its roof. It's golden now, isn't it? And the sky green between the masts?"[8]

The narrator takes off his glasses to see the colors more clearly and comments that her dark glasses have given distortion to the colors, too. When she takes off her spectacles, he sees for the first time her china-blue eyes. Romantic yearning comes over him rapidly. Her confession that she does not love her husband makes his wishful thinking tenable. But, being a true romantic, he is not comfortable with the thought that he will win his lady easily. Like Faust, who yearns for the most beautiful woman in the world and admires her mutely from afar, the typical Sansom protagonist in these stories prefers detachment and fantasies to emotional involvement.

As she smiles at him vacantly, he slowly realizes that her smile is not that of a nymphomaniac but of a blind woman with eyes of glass. Then she tells him the terrible story of her blinding by her husband in a drunken rage of jealousy with a broken bottle. She says she must stay with her husband because all he lives for is to make it up to her.

Although she does not believe in forgiveness or forgetting, she explains why she cannot leave him. "He'd think I had gone away to leave him free. He'd think I was unburdening him. He'd have no more way of making up for what he did. He'd be left alone with his conscience . . . I could never do that to him."[9] She also adds that she cannot leave Trondhjem because it is the only place she can still "see."

They lunch together and explore the city through her "eyes." When they part she raises her face to the brilliant tall Christmas tree in the square. Its frosted light flashes on her glasses and she speaks of candles. He doesn't dare ask her if she has seen that the candles are electric now.

They part. He boards the ship home to England. While he remembers the girl's beauty and humility, two English businessmen at the bar compare their watches with the clock on the way and say goodbye to the North. When one says, "We gain an hour," the narrator loses his temper and smashes his fist in the businessman's face.

Ostensibly this melodramatic ending expresses the narrator's anger at the superiority of his fellow Britisher over the Norwegians. Actually, it supplies the explanation for the opening paragraph of the story which describes the narrator's feelings in a jail cell. But such a melodramatic ending to an already bizarre, Poe-like story of the beautiful woman being blinded seems gratuitous. The woman's moral integrity and special sensibilities render the terrible beauty of the setting and her own blind inner beauty very well. Had Sansom ended the story with a wistful goodbye to her and the North, the total effect of the story would have been improved.

Another story, "The Girl on the Bus," adds to the reader's knowledge of Sansom's romantic observer. It begins:

> Since to love is better than to be loved, unrequited love may be the finest love of all. If this is so, then the less requited the finer. And it follows that the most refined passion possible for us must finally be for those to whom we have never even spoken, whom we have never met. The passing face, the anguish of a vision of a face sitting alone in front of you so endearing and so moving and so beautiful that you are torn and sick inside with hope and despair, instant despair . . . for it is hopelessly plain that no word can ever be spoken, those eyes will never greet yours, in a few minutes the bell will ring, the bus will shudder to a stop, and down some impersonal side street she will be gone. Never to be seen again.[10]

Here again is the theme of Faustian yearning for the unknown but beautiful that recurs in almost all the stories in *The Passionate North* and in later stories. The unhappy endings that Sansom would never risk in his novels occur often in his short stories and render them more interesting than the novels just because of the surprise element. In "The Girl on the Bus," the protagonist Harry is touring Haga Park on foot when a beautiful woman on skis passes by. He catches only two long ski-strides' worth of her and he is breathless.

That night, alone in his hotel dining room, he begins to worry. The nature of his thoughts gives us insight into Sansom:

> The sight of that girl has coloured my whole life. By a hundredth chance I was in Stockholm . . . and I had to see *her*. Now forever I am left with a standard of beauty which my world will always slightly fail. My relationships with women will never seem quite so keen, all other pursuits will seem henceforth without quite so much purpose. Of course, I shall enjoy myself in degree. But

perfection has been trifled with. This kind of thing goes deeper than one thinks. . . . Oh why in hell did I go to Haga? . . . And it is not as if I was as young as I was.[11]

Obsessed by the thought of this unobtainable woman, he travels around Sweden. Finally, in Denmark, he boards a train for Esbjaerg and England. At the Great Belt the train boards a ferry for the overnight trip.

To his surprise, the girl from Haga is on board. He sees her in the salon serenely writing a letter and, at one point, looking straight at him, frowning. But he lacks courage to approach her. Instead he becomes seasick as the boat lurches through a storm.

When he feels better the next day he looks for her in the smoke-room. ". . . The long tossing day stretched out grey and eventless. . . . To be sick is dreadful, but to spend a day lurching among lurching things, with never a level moment, is if not unendurable of the deepest, most troublesome tedium."[12] From the experience of writing *The Equilibriad* a few years before, Sansom learned how to blend loss of balance with the setting and emotions.

The narrator never gains the courage to talk to her, but when the boat docks and he sees her with an old man, she speaks to him. She remembers him from Haga and asks him to help her and her father. They have lost their seat reservations on the train to London.

They never stop talking on the train and they marry at the end, with Harry never regretting his inability to speak to her first.

Two other stories in the volume depict this same solitary traveler. In "Gliding Gulls and Going People" the traveler is so intent on picking up a woman that he is impervious to the Scottish sights he is passing. In "Time and Place" the man whose last name is Rose is caught in a fog with a young woman who is staying at the same hotel in Mull, an island off Scotland. The mist encloses them for a brief sexual encounter. The emptiness of the day is what brought them together; their relationship is casual. This story integrates mood and setting well.

III   A Touch of the Sun

In most of the stories in *A Touch of the Sun*, the protagonist lives a moment of nightmare, real or imagined. While *The Passionate North* marked progress from *South* in terms of better integration of story with place, *A Touch of the Sun* marks the influence of Ivan Bunin in the gentle comic rendering of characters. Bunin, in "The Gentleman from San Francisco," created a man puffed up from business success and an inability to grasp his own gaucherie. So too is Sansom's Ludwig De Broda of "Episode at Gastein."

In "Episode at Gastein" Ludwig De Broda, a middle-aged aristocratic roué, meets young Fraulein Laure Perfuss. A humorous May-December romance ensues. But while he debates over whether she is worthy of his name, she meets a younger man who wins her hand.

The structure is based on giving Ludwig's and Laure's views alternately. In particular, there is a double shot of a scene in which both are in their baths at the same time, thinking of each other. De Broda muses on her interest in films and its possible implications in terms of their incompatibility.

> "Come, come," de Broda thought. "Don't let's be intolerant. Don't let's us be hurried. It was only a lapse—why, in any case, shouldn't she like the films? A young girl has her interests. There are very good films, too. Sometimes. She was really most charming. . . ." And alone there his lips parted in a wide smile he remembered the pleasant feelings he had, the expanded sense of himself. . . . "Vanity!" he said sternly. He stared hard at his big toe sticking up as from a separate body. There were several long black hairs streaming down beneath the nail. "Why!" he thought in wonder, "I've never noticed *those* before."[13]

His vanity is so pervasive that he does not realize her impatience for action and life. He fools himself into thinking he will mold her taste to his, which is largely based upon nostalgia for the past aristocratic world into which he had been born.

While he is pondering the right time to propose to her, she, in her bath, is thinking:

> . . . "He's different, all right." She grimaced. ". . . He'd be a credit. I can just see him at the head of the table, a party for just six. . . ." And her mind crept about silver candlesticks, a glitter of glasses, and the form of de Broda across the polished table with his polished manners so ably discoursing—he inclined a little forward to the lady seated on his right. That lady too inclined forward, her eyes never leaving his face. . . . Laure rose with an abrupt splash and began soaping herself severely. "As for *her* . . ." she muttered decisively.[14]

She is approaching thirty and wants to find a husband on this holiday. She is willing to mold de Broda's taste to hers without realizing exactly how arrogant he is about his family lines.

But a young Swiss acts faster than de Broda. Laure quickly transfers her interest from de Broda to the Swiss, much to the bewilderment of de Broda. It takes him a while to understand her preference for such a young man. But gradually he realizes that they embody the simple tale of "youth to youth." He thinks first of suicide by jumping from a bridge and then he decides slitting his wrists in the bath is more suitable. When he draws his warm bath and readies the razor blades, he finds that his characteristic indecisiveness stops him. As he ponders his fear of decision, he abruptly realizes why Laure has chosen the Swiss over him. It is a reason based on de Broda's own values, not Laure's: he believes she has chosen the Swiss because of Swiss francs, which are all powerful. He therefore rationalizes that the potency of the Swiss is not sexual but financial.

As he imagines the young couple skiing together into the horizon, waving to him and laughing, he realizes he is once again all alone without hope. The last paragraph describes a pathetic scene.

De Broda sat absolutely still in the hot water, a little razor-blade held in each hand like the parts of a child's broken toy. And slowly two tears, two big single tears dropped from his eyes, dribbled over his cheeks, and fell down into the other water beneath.[15]

Once again, his vanity emerges. This time it sustains him. In this tragicomic ending Sansom reveals de Broda's true nature—he is a detached romantic observer happier in his lonely life than he would ever be as a man with a life's companion.

IV *Summary of the Travel Short Stories*

With the travel–short story, Sansom has created a unique form. Each of the three volumes of travel stories treats eloquently setting and character. Sansom uses setting as a foil to character. At times, he shows his taste for the bizarre in characters and plots that the form of the short story allows him to sketch at Poe's "white heat." At other times, he filters setting through plot with a Proustian memory for sensuous details. Probably the most constant element in these stories and a sign of a new confidence in characterization is his ability to create "the absurd" with the comic spirit of Bunin. These stories succeed not only as travel stories but as literature.

CHAPTER 5

The Short Stories

CONCOMITANT with the publication of novels and travel assignments, Sansom wrote numerous short stories that have been collected in a dozen volumes. Since some stories appear in more than one collection, I shall refer to individual stories rather than to collections.

Sansom's greatest talents lie in his short stories. Elizabeth Bowen, in the introduction to *The Stories of William Sansom,* praises his talents. She says,

> Here is a writer whose faculties not only suit the short story but are suited by it—suited and, one may feel, enhanced. This form needs the kind of imagination which is able to concentrate at high power. . . . The tension and pace required by the short story can be as stimulating to the right writer of it as they are intimidating to the wrong one: evidently they are stimulating to William Sansom. . . . There is also the necessity to project, to make seen, and make seen with significance—the short story is for the eye (if the mind's eye). Also the short story, though it highlights what appears to be reality, is not— cannot wish or afford to be—realistic: it relies on devices, foreshortenings, "effects." In the narration there must be an element of conjury, and of that William Sansom is an evident master.[1]

Compared with his novels, which are uneven in form, his short stories are uniformly successful. He has himself expressed greater enjoyment in writing short stories than novels. They seem to be more suitable to his watchful eye and do not demand the depth of exploration of human psyche. Stories also capture these words of his: "A writer lives best, in a state of astonishment. Beneath any feeling he has of the good or the evil of the world lies a deeper one of wonder. . . ."[2]

While the ambiguities of illusion versus reality found in *Fireman Flower* remain a viable theme, Sansom explores many other themes. I have selected stories representative of recurrent themes on revenge, fear and violence, marriage, friendship and death, challenges to

Sansom, societal issues, and two stories that are his favorites. These themes are often refracted by Sansom's narrator who is both detached and romantic. Usually the detached side of his personality wins because he would rather yearn for something or someone and be unfulfilled than forced into active participation in life.

I Stories of Revenge

A story that combines the theme of revenge with humor is "A Contest of Ladies," the title story from a collection published in 1956. It is about a May-December relationship.

Fred Morley, an eccentric, wealthy bachelor finds himself host to six beauty queens who have come to his home in a Channel Island resort town for a beauty contest. Immediately he picks out Miss Great-Belt of Denmark as the most beautiful and most disaffected by his charms.

At the same time he is enjoying the intimacy of the beauty queens, he observes their strange beauty routines.

He had found Miss Clermont-Ferrand sitting with her head in her beautiful hands and each elbow cupped in the half of a lemon. Across the landing there had whisked a blue kimono topped by a face plastered livid dry pink, with hollows it seemed where the eyes might be and naked lips huge now as a clown's, a face terribly faceless—too late he had seen that this might be Miss Great-Belt. Then Miss Rotterdam, in a bathing dress, had come bumping across the landing on her bottom, and vanished into the bathroom: no hands nor legs, she had explained *en route*—a question of stomach muscles. Miss Sauerkraut liked to lie on the balcony on half a ping-pong table, head-downwards. Miss Civitavecchia he had found carefully combing the long black beards that hung from her armpits, a peninsula specialty; unlike Miss Amsterdam who took no such Latin pride in the strong growth of dark hair that covered most of her—it seemed that whenver he asked for her the answer came: "Upstairs shaving."[3]

Sansom revels in the comic description of external beauty and is at his best in this story when describing that aspect of women. Five years later, when he returns to this subject in *The Last Hours of Sandra Lee,* he no longer handles it with the same lightness.

While Fred subtly arranges a dinner date with Miss Great-Belt, he takes two other queens out at noon. But Miss Great-Belt never appears at their rendezvous. Later when he confronts her at home, she casually gives the excuse that to dine and sit all night in a cramped theater box with the contest coming up the next morning is not appealing.

To Fred's hurt response at her breaking the date, she chastises him for his licentious behavior in taking advantage of the women at his home.

"Well *really.* You spend the morning with not one but *two* of these . . . these *women* upstairs. And then you expect to spend the evening with *me?* What do you think I am? What next? Shall I tell you waht *you* are—you're an old satyr, that is what. A wolf! With pointed ears! With hoofs!"[4]

She delivers the word "hoofs" with a mouth shaped for "whoofing" down whole houses. Fred does not take this accurate portrayal of himself gracefully. He vows revenge. And he can carry it out easily because, unbeknown to her, he is one of the judges of the beauty contest.

The next day at the contest hall, Miss Great-Belt loses all her composure when she sees Fred in the judges' stand. Her first reaction is anger at herself for being so stupid as to tell him off. Then she condemns him as a monster for not having told her that he would be a judge. But her fears are allayed by the thought that he will be sorry for his deception and, because deep-down he is really in love with her, he will vote for her. She also feels that even if he does not, there are four other judges who will surely see how much more beautiful she is than the other women.

But she is wrong. Fred not only votes against her but persuades everyone to do so also. His vanity has been too bruised by her attack to vote objectively.

When she hears the decision, she is wildly upset. She thinks of setting his house on fire, accusing him of rape, and assaulting him. But then she decides on a calmer, more vengeful act: she will flirt with him, woo him, and marry him. And she does.

Fred is triumphant at the end and innocent of his bride's vengeance. But the reader is aware of the lifelong tortures Miss Great-Belt will invent for him. The ending is contrived, though it does make an interesting reversal of the usual power-struggle between man and woman. Sansom has given her the ability to see Fred as he is and the self-confidence to do battle against him. On the one hand, these abilities seem to warrant her abandonment of Fred and progress to another more worthy challenge. But, on the other hand, Sansom may well be describing the love-hate magnetism of two people bent on winning each other at whatever the cost.

Another story of revenge, "A Last Word," published in *A Contest of Ladies* and later in *The Stories of William Sansom,* succeeds in being humorous even though it ends in a funeral. The revenge is between a landlord, Henry Cadwaller, and his tenant, Horton.

Cadwaller is parsimonious and Horton proves to be his main irritant both as a tenant and a friend; thereby, Horton becomes the stimulus of Cadwaller's life. When Cadwaller sets the overflow-holes in the bathtub three inches lower to save on water bills, Horton covers them with a sponge so he can enjoy a full tub. Cadwaller serves his guests food half-raw to save gas but Horton constantly sends his food back to the cook to be burnt! Although Cadwaller has made a no-cooking rule in the rooms, the odor of cooking always seeps through Horton's door. Try as Cadwaller does, he never finds a gas-ring, for Horton cooks beneath a tent of sheets on an electric blanket.

As they age together, they become companions, lunching together or going to a pub together. At lunch if one is served a larger helping, there are nasty words. Eventually they learn to order different dishes and suffer only if they see huger helpings at other tables. In the pub, Cadwaller orders three mild beers, inexpensive and worthwhile in terms of drinking time. Horton orders a small whiskey in a large glass, enjoying Cadwaller's discomfiture over all the free soda water that goes with the whiskey.

From his thrift of walking around in shoes with soles "the size of the yolk of a flat-fried egg," Cadwaller contracts bronchitis. He refuses fires and hot-water bottles so that, in effect, he kills himself. Bereft of his adversary, Horton appears to others as an old little boy left out of the game with no one to play with. He is seen digging up a bush in the garden before Cadwaller's funeral. His shoulders shake and everyone wonders if he is weeping.

At the end of the short funeral service, Horton is the last one to place his bush on the grave. People see him walk away, a solitary figure "into the years of loneliness. . . . Nobody . . . saw the giant chuckle beneath Mr. Horton's bowed shoulders: nobody knew the true nature of his last tribute, his bloom, his last word, *Rubus Idaeus,* the common raspberry."[5]

Thus Horton gains revenge over his companion by the humorous transformation of a school boy's "raspberry" cheer into an adult horticultural pun. The ending like the rest of the story has a subtle and comic effect that are superior to some of the moralistic endings of Sansom's earlier stories.

II   *Stories of Fear and Violence*

While Sansom deplored violence in the media because he felt man was nine-tenths parrot, he occasionally wrote about men full of physical violence or with the potential for it. Although "Various Temptations" originally appeared in *Something Terrible, Something Lovely* in 1948 and "Among the Dahlias" in *Among the Dahlias* in 1957, and both were chosen eventually by Sansom for his collection *The Stories of William Sansom* in 1963, they share a common theme. Both are concerned with a willing victim who passively awaits victimization. Several years later, Muriel Spark, another fine British writer, also chose this theme in her novella *The Driver's Seat*.

Clara in "Various Temptations" and Doole in "Among the Dahlias" appear to be ordinary people content with their humdrum lives. Then into their lives comes an overwhelming force: in "Various Temptations," the force is an insane strangler; in "Among the Dahlias," the force is a lion let loose from his cage in the zoo.

Each character meets her/his fate with a certain perversity. Clara, a plain woman and invisible mender by occupation, lies in her lonely bed with the window open. She is invisible to most people not only by virtue of her occupation but by virtue of her common, bland appearance. She knows a strangler has already murdered four women in her neighborhood. But since the newspapers equate the strangler with Jack the Ripper, who chose prostitutes as his victims, Clara feels both comforted and rejected.

... Clara put the paper down—thinking, well for one thing she never did herself up like those sort, in fact she never did herself up at all, and what would be the use? Instinctively then she turned to look across to the mirror on the dressing-table, saw there her worn pale face and sack-coloured hair, and felt instantly neglected; down in her plain-feeling body there stirred again that familiar envy, the impotent grudge that still came to her at least once every day of her life—that nobody had ever bothered to think deeply for her, neither loving, not hating, nor in any way caring.[6]

Similarly Doole, on his lunch hour, strolls through the zoo and encounters an uncaged lion. He thinks,

O, God, please save me.... If only it could speak, if only like all these animals in books it could *speak,* then I could tell it how I'm me and how I must go on living, and about my house and my showroom.... I'm not just meat, I'm a person, a club-member, a goldfish-feeder, a lover of flowers and detective-stories—and I'll promise to reduce that profit on fire-surrounds, I promise from forty to thirty percent. I'd have to some day anyway, but won't make excuses any more. . . . Two separate feelings predominated: one, an athletic, almost youthful alertness—as though he could make his body spring everywhere at once and at superlative speed; the other, an over-powering knowledge of guilt—and with it the canny hope that somehow he could bargain his way out, somehow expiate his wrong and avoid punishment. He had experienced this dual sensation before at moments in business when he had something to hide, and in some way hid the matter more securely by confessing half of his culpability.[7]

He is desperate to be spared so he is willing to admit to anything.

Clara is "chosen" by Ron Raikes, the strangler. He enters through her window and wins her sympathy by sitting on her bed and talking to her. Even he, with his killer instincts, senses something is wrong. She is not struggling for her life and thus does not agitate him to quell her. She also appears to be unattractive.

He moves in with her, living in her sitting room, and soon they plan to marry. When she returns one day with a surprise birthday present for him, two ties, six yards of white material for her bridal gown, and a box of thin red candles, she muses on Ron's strange attractiveness. He seems interested in his own safèty but also is preoccupied with her as no one ever has been. Starved for attention, she willingly risks her life. Subconsciously she knows he is dangerous. Consciously, she decides, just this once for his surprise birthday tea, to make herself look pretty. And here is her fatal error. She paints her lips with a thick scarlet smear. She hears Ron opening the door and lights a red candle to give a festive air. To him, she now resembles the kind of women who have been his victims. He observes that

. . . her face seemed to be charged with light, expressive, and, in its new self-assurance, predatory. It was a face bent on effect, on making its mischief. Instinctively it performed new tricks, attitudes learnt and stored but never before used, the intuitive mimicry of the female seducer. . . . The trouble roasted on his brain.[8]

He ends his observation by leaning toward her as if to clown and kiss her. Instead, he takes the ties she has brought as a gift and strangles her.

On the other hand, Doole, in "Among the Dahlias," is never attacked by the lion.

... [Instead the lion] did something which was probably ... worse for Doole: certainly worse for his peace of mind, which would have been properly at peace had his body gone, but which was now left forever afterwards to suffer from a shock peculiar to the occasion. If we are not animals, if the human mind is superior to the simple animal body, then it must be true to say that by not being killed, Doole finally suffered a greater ill.[9]

Doole suffers rejection, rejection by a lion who does not consider him fit to devour. Why is Doole disappointed that he has not been chosen as a victim? Evidently his mundane life, like Clara's, holds no excitement for him. He feels alone and undesirable.

The ending is a teaser. Doole partly recovers his nerve and begins to look at himself in the mirror with an eye to self-improvement. He has his teeth fixed, visits a Turkish bath regularly with the intention of losing his old self by sweating, and he begins to run long distances regularly. Does he do it to run away from himself or from something?

In both stories, Sansom mixes pathos with comedy. Clara is overjoyed to be wanted by someone, even if that someone is a criminal known for strangling women. Her gaiety at the end of the story as she assumes Ron is clowning but is actually strangling her diminishes into little noises. These noises suggest both frightened resistance and disbelief. Doole never became more actively involved in life than after rejection by the lion. His meanness as a businessman used to distract him from self-realization. But once his life has been spared he no longer is able to lose himself in his usual pettiness. He appears to be forever after confronted with the big question of why the lion found him wanting.

Like the fearful Doole, Mervyn Tressiter in "To the Rescue," published in *Among the Dahlias*, tries to be heroic but fails. He sees a boy drowning in the ocean. Though he is a weak swimmer, he swims out to try to save him. Halfway there, he decides he does not know how to rescue the boy so that he will probably drown with him. He turns around and starts to dog-paddle back to shore.

Meanwhile an old man bounds into the ocean and saves the boy. As the man gives the boy artificial respiration, Tressiter stands by expecting to be congratulated for having gone to rescue the boy. ". . . The lie had formed in him, he had never really turned back, he had gone in after the boy and risked his life, he who was a poor swimmer had done this."[10] But the man ignores Tressiter and takes the boy to a nearby hut. He slams the door on Tressiter's offer to get brandy.

Tressiter stands on the porch feeling sorry for himself, his wet clothes, and the lack of recognition of his brave act. Like Doole, he has been found wanting in courage—whether it is courage to be chosen by a lion or to be drowned in a vain rescue. Also like Doole, he can lie to himself until the reality of rejection by the outside world obtrudes itself.

Fear and violence are combined within the persona of the same individual in "The Man with the Moon in Him," published in *Among the Dahlias.* A nameless man, affected by the full moon, goes out for a lonely walk. He follows a heavily painted girl up the stairs to a train. But he does not follow her into the train. Instead, he waits for the doors to slam shut and for the train to depart. Then he takes out a pencil stub from his pocket. With it he writes quickly in the white space of an advertisement in large letters a single obscene word.

Then he drops the stub into his pocket. In between arrivals and departures of trains, he repeats the act of writing the obscene word on other advertisements. At one point, he is defacing a poster of a girl in a low-cut dress. His stub slips from his hand and falls near the live-voltage rail. Frustrated, he leaves the station.

Soon he sees a young woman smelling of soap and scent. He follows her through a park. As she disappears behind a bush, holding a package of fish she has just purchased, he leaps at her from behind.

. . . She made no sound but for a little sob deep inside her open mouth. The fish in its newspaper fell squashed between them. He butted her face up with his chin and looked close into her eyes. . . . She stared up at him with the innocence of a child about to be struck . . . with all the strange love of victim for assailant.[11]

Her look and attitude so disarm him that his hands drop to his sides. As she presses her pocketbook on him, he says gauchely the first thing that enters his mind: "'A pencil . . . could you please lend me . . . a pencil?' before she fell, in a dead faint, to the ground."[12]

Sansom has deftly transposed a primitive man who is repressed and bored into a marshmallow. The comic effect brings relief after the tension that has been built, and the twist of violence diminishing into fear rather than fear accelerating into violence, as in the works of Poe, is a clever device.

III   *Stories of Marriage*

While most of Sansom's novels focus on romance and young married couples, his short stories from 1957 on, concomitant with his own aging process, deal with middle-aged crises. He can render the bristle of two people concisely and effectively. Elizabeth Bowen views the underlying theme of these stories as one of resignation and reconciliation. Often the catalyst is a forbidding landscape that both alienates the couple and brings them together.

"A Waning Moon," although originally published in *The Passionate North*, a travel book, was included in *The Stories of William Sansom* because it is a vivid example of the conflict of a middle-aged couple with themselves, each other, and the landscape. The story opens with a woman's scream in the night in a deserted place. Nearby is a caravan or mobile home with a man inside.

Through flashback Sansom recounts how the woman, Ruth Rose, came to be screaming out for help. She and her husband are on a caravan holiday in the Highlands. In the beginning, the moon was full but some nights later it is on the wane and its weakening force seems to affect the atmosphere. It affects the couple, too. They argue as they make camp in the darkness.

As they settle in, he goes out for water while she cooks supper. When he returns, they discuss what they can decipher of the dark landscape around them. She says it looks like scree, jagged and loose. While eating dinner he writes in his journal that they are in slate-quarrying country. Tension mounts as he withdraws into his notebook and Ruth pours herself a large glass of whiskey. She goads him further.

... Draining the whiskey she raised again her voice and repeated and repeated what she knew he had heard before. Beginning to move with it too, swaying on her seat, thumping the table, turning on with one flat sharp stroke the wireless switch, flooding thus the caravan with sound against his silence—so that again he moved his hand wearily across his forehead. And suddenly she wrenched herself up, pulling at the same time the table-cloth, crashing down plates and food and the mess of gravy, shaking the caravan, screaming. ... She took up a tea-pot and threw it against the wall, and as so much sound and violence crashed away out of her that same very need for finality overtook her own senses, the known act was flushed over with hysteria, the room took charge mounting into a headache and a blackening of light—until she could only get to the door and fling open and, screaming, bundle down the steps into the night air.[13]

The atmosphere assumes the shape of anger in this anthropomorphic paragraph. It sends Ruth out into the misty land where she wanders through a forbidden gate. She finds herself bounded by a precipice and a still mineral lake to which she is magnetically drawn. Whether she slips into the quarry-lake or, in a trance, jumps in is unknown.

As she hits the icy water, her scream reaches her husband's ears as he sits sulking inside the caravan. He rushes to her rescue and, at great peril, saves her from drowning. When she recovers her senses, she rebukes him with her old bitterness. He tries to calm her down and steer her away from the lake. But he is suddenly struck by a violent thought. No one saw him go there. He could loosen his grip on her and let her fall back into the quarry. "He . . . looked for the last time round that basin of loneliness. Then, quite suddenly, she raised her free hand and made a gesture to move the hair from her eyes, to smooth open her brow. A movement well-known to him, simple, a gesture both efficient and helplessly feminine."[14]

This feminine gesture saves her and him. Despite his wife's temper, he feels compassion for her and knows they must live out their lives together and accept the loneliness they feel at times as part of the human condition. Sansom makes the husband believable. He is a man with a sense of proportion. But Ruth, in her jealous isolation, resembles some of the shrill characters from his novels. Her jealousy and temper tantrums endanger her life. Once saved from drowning, she displays no capacity to relent or change; thus she becomes a stereotype of a virago.

"The Dangerous Age," published in *Among the Dahlias*, is an amusing story about a middle-aged couple whose problem begins when the wife, Janet Orde, decides that, with the onslaught of middle-age, she must create some illusions of youth. She changes all the bright bulbs in their home to forty-watt bulbs. This softens her wrinkles and assures her that her husband, Bertram, will not be tempted by the dangerous age to philander.

When Bertram comes home, his reactions to the new ambience are not what she expected.

"Funny," he said, "feels a bit foggy in here. Didn't notice it outside. Chimney been smoking?"

"No, dear."

"Well, I don't know," he said. He looked round the room, sniffing, his teeth bared in that ever-fixed smile. Then he went over to the wine-cupboard. Fingering for glasses, he stumbled in the corner among darkly shiny walnut. "I'm going blind," he muttered. . . .

Quite brightly, as if it had just occurred to her, she added:

"I've changed the bulbs—did you notice? The lights are softer."

"So *that's* it!" he said and looked over to his own chair. "But can we read?"

"It's these dreadful headaches," she said, turning her big dark eyes on him, letting her mouth quiver a little. "These bright lights *split* my head right open."[15]

Bertram is sympathetic and privately resolves to buy himself a spotlight reading lamp. But he does not.

Increasingly he finds it difficult to read at home. Since he is too vain to buy glasses, he holds the reading matter in his hands but finds his thoughts wandering dangerously.

He was sitting, with the yellow lights, with Janet's flat bosom, with the frilled beige blouse, the long droop of pearls.

"You look like an old dog," he said to her silently, "a collie." And in the next second, thought: "But you're my own dear collie, my Janet whom I courted at sweet twenty-three." . . . He was very fond of Janet.[15]

While he contemplates pursuit of other women, Janet feels that the lowered lights have made her look more beautiful. She does not realize that he can no longer see her except as a blur in that darkened, dead room.

One day when Bertram mistakenly picks up a golfball for his sherry glass, he decides to get eye glasses. Janet greets his decision with mixed feelings. She figures that, if his eyes are weakening, then even in sharp daylight she will be protected from too sharp scrutiny.

Getting glasses spurs him to seek a new woman because glasses are further proof of his disintegration. So he gathers up courage and meets a Miss Eglinton in a railway station. Eventually he is lying to Janet about needing to work late at the office. Janet believes him and derives comfort from knowing he is earning extra money for the future in case he goes blind. The story ends with the following ironic lines: "Alone among her soft furnishings she suddenly felt like Lucrezia Borgia. Deliciously. But guiltily too."[17]

Sansom's tone in this story is controlled and objective. He pokes fun at Janet for sacrificing reality for the illusion of youth and he pokes fun at Bertram for sacrificing his youthful vigor and fidelity, pre-lowered-lights stage of life, for the reality of middle-aged decline. Janet's illusion *becomes* Bertram's reality. Ironically, each seems satisfied with the exchange. Their middle-aged battle of the sexes is gently mocked with very comical results.

Less comic and more sardonic is another story written fifteen years later and contained in Sansom's last collection. "The Marmalade Bird," title story of the collection published in 1973, focuses on Henry

and Margaret Livingstone, middle-aged and vacationing in Marra-
kech. Through the years they have learned to accommodate themselves to each other's selfishness. They magnify each other's gestures
and finickyness in a new twist to the illusion versus reality theme of
the early fireman stories. The illusions of the fireman stories have
been described by William York Tindall as follows:

. . . These delirious visions of firemen in the intricate warehouse of maze,
potting-shed, and occupants, and of the leg-roasting beauty seem portentous
allegories but, like dreams, remain unclear. Fear is the principal emotion, the
machinery is Freud's, and the manner is Freud's and the manner is
persuasively matter-of-fact. [18]

In contrast, the Livingstones' illusions are not tantalizing and not
portentous allegories. Their illusions, like most of the illusions of the
characters of Sansom's later short stories, help them survive in a
reality that is also more awesome than the reality of the characters
from the fireman stories. This contrast emphasizes the change of the
young Sansom, full of belief in the force of illusion to the middle-aged
Sansom, disenchanted with illusion and concentrating on the here-
and-now.

Awesome reality to the Livingstones is centered upon a small bird,
a tabib, that first roosts on the window sill of their hotel room and
later gets its head stuck in their marmalade pot. When the tabib
begins flying around their breakfast table, its long beak pecking at the
marmalade left on the dishes, Margaret is amused while Henry is
annoyed. Actually, the bird supplies a reason for them to snap at each
other. Being on vacation and sharing a happy sex life, they have no
major irritations and so they need to invent some. A Freudian may be
able to supply reasons for this need; Sansom does not. He simply
accepts the daily bickering of a long-married couple as a part of
marriage.

When they find a tabib roosting on their shutter at night, Margaret
wants to leave it alone but Henry wants her to close the shutter
because of the mosquitoes. She wins the argument. Soon they are
covered by mosquitoes.

Henry puts toothpaste on his face to act as a mosquito repellent.
It doesn't help. So he rises in the middle of the night mumbling that he
is St. Francis of Assisi and silently lowers the shutter, thus risking the
fall of the tabib to its death.

The next morning, Margaret accuses him of killing the bird. When
it does not arrive for its ration of marmalade, she covers the pot with

Kleenex. Then suddenly the bird flies in. It plunges its long beak into the pot and never comes up. The beak is stuck in the wad of Kleenex.

Each yells at the other to help the bird. A tall Senegalese servant appears to witness the comical scene.

This man stood for a moment more astonished by humans than by bird: by the doctor's malevolent bloodhound eye and ghostly face patched with white toothpaste, by the wife with hair pinned mannishly down in a nightnet. But his second thought, as servant and nationality host to these strangers from the white North, was to be of assistance to the poor crazed things.[19]

Henry, though a doctor who is supposed to revere life, moves to toss the bird over the balcony. But his wife grabs the bird and delicately wrenches its beak out of the pot. Henry is shocked at this self-sacrifice. He never thought she would risk dirtying her hands and being bitten.

The bird with mashed Kleenex and marmalade rind on its beak says, "Taa-bib," which for a moment sounded like "Thank you." This sudden two-syllable acknowledgment of kindness and abnegation of selfishness draws the husband and wife together in an embrace.

The scavenger bird that preys on the sweets of others suggests both the husband and wife unconsciously preying on each other's nerves. But, in a crisis, they reveal sensitivity and care not only for the pitiful bird but also for each other.

Another story of marriage written later in Sansom's life is "Love at First Sight," published in *The Marmalade Bird*. It is very short and focuses on the love Richard and Mona Lister feel for each other at first sight aboard ship on a holiday. What is unusual about this view of a married couple is Sansom's laying bare the illusion each had about the other and showing them in search of that person for the rest of their lives.

Mona first sees Richard's face framed in a porthole, eyes gazing intently at hers as she stands on a higher deck. To her, his eyes are "visionary, rhapsodic, lost." To him, her face is also framed by a porthole and fits his particular dream of a girl.

They meet and marry. And Richard never again looks so beatific as he did that first time. The tender sensibility of the blush he had shown is not to be found in the Richard she married. "He was predatory and materialistic, an engineer by profession—though, of course, . . . he had . . . his romantic moments."[20] What Mona does not know is that at the time she saw him, he was in the men's room passing water and idly looking through the porthole. Unlike the couples from Sansom's earlier romantic stories and novels, the Listers do not live happily ever after. Duped by their initial reactions, they never achieve the soulful intimacy they thought each would give the other.

IV   Stories about Friendship and Death

The Ulcerated Milkman, published in 1966, contains the short story of the same name, "The Ulcerated Milkman," which is one of Sansom's most comic and pathetic stories. Unfortunately, it has never been included in any other collections published outside of England.

Bradshaw, the protagonist, is a milkman who loathes milk while exhorting others to drink it. He goes from doorway to doorway praying for a plague of "great tits." Meanwhile the milk company announces a contest. For the milkman who increases sales the most in a three-month period, there will be a prize of a motor scooter. He works hard at winning but begins to spit blood from ulcers.

Soon he is hospitalized and told the cure for his ulcers is—milk! Disgruntled, nostalgic for stout, he and Brown, the elderly patient in the next bed, eat semolina and junket with milk while reciting a litany of potatoes *à la français* and other forbidden foods. They vie with each other to produce menus spicy, hot, and dangerous to their health.

After Bradshaw returns from an X-ray, he tells Brown about a dream he had while drugged. It is a humorous dream blending both forbidden foods and women, particularly the pretty nurses.

Them Yanks with their specs and ulcers, tired out by their computors [sic], flaked off with their hamburgers and martinis—when they go to this club like good old Elks and sit around while a bird with long nylons and big fluffy ears comes and listens to their troubles, while they take a refreshing scotch-on-the-rocks. They don't touch this bird. See what I mean?[21]

The nurses appear to him as bunnies and everyone seems more privileged than he and Brown. Brown is appreciative of Bradshaw's humor and imagination. But the reverse is not true. Bradshaw takes Brown's presence for granted. As Bradshaw's health improves he becomes insensitive to Brown's feelings. Brown's fantasies about foods irk Bradshaw because they are no longer forbidden to him.

One day Brown has a violent hemorrhage and is taken out of the room. Bradshaw does not see him leave because he is making the rounds of the rooms to boast about the motor scooter he has won in the contest. When he returns to the room and learns that Brown has died, he is remorseful for his rudeness.

As he returns to normal life and delivers milk on his scooter, he thinks of the hospital as the place of golden days and wishes he could drive old Brown down to the coast on his free days.

Michel-Michot feels the balance of tragedy with comedy in this story "is disturbing because it does not emerge from the story itself but is contrived by Sansom to bring into relief the other side of reality at all costs."[22] But she is perhaps overlooking the unreality patients feel in hospitals and the ensuing euphoria of feeling better that makes them egotistical. Sansom, having had ulcers himself, understands these feelings well. The emptiness Bradshaw faces when he recovers and realizes his loss of a dear friend seems entirely realistic and plausible. Thus the story is memorable for its depiction of a tender relationship between men.

V *A Story Sansom Regretted Having Written*

One story Sansom regretted ever writing is "The Last Ride," published in *Among the Dahlias.* It is about a beloved uncle's funeral at a crematorium. The narrator is Nennie, a niece of Uncle Jack, who is considered the "queer one" of the family. Proof of her queerness, she feels, is in her looking forward to Uncle Jack's cremation. ". . . Although she had been deeply affected when Uncle Jack died, she had cried herself to sleep, she felt in some other compartment of her strange mind that he was still alive and intent on giving them all an interesting and unusual day out. She knew he was dead all right, but half her mind was still able to think otherwise."[23]

While the priest is praying over the coffin, Nennie believes Uncle Jack would have roared at the solemnity of all the friends and relatives gathered round. But, when the priest finishes and the coffin moves off mysteriously of its own accord toward the brass doors that swing open to receive it, everyone sighs with either relief or sadness.

The dead coffin of its own accord came to life and moved off. Dreams of furniture on the move became real, the dreadful advance of wardrobes came for a moment true. The coffin slid off by itself on a secret mechanical voyage.

The great brass doors opened like the petals of a hungry plant to receive their long polished food foot by foot—until only the last of it remained, and then this too disappeared, and Uncle Jack had gone at last. With ruthless finality, the gates closed.[24]

Nennie is tempted to applaud the "entertainment." Everyone looks uncomfortable. That night in her diary Nennie writes about Uncle Jack's last gay ride with appreciation.

In retrospect, Sansom felt that the story had questionable morals but did not elucidate. Whether his own mother's recent death had caused him to criticize "The Last Ride" or whether the story had been criticized by others for its callousness is open to conjecture.[25]

VI   *Challenges*

Sansom enjoyed challenges. He once read in a brochure about a school of writing whose cardinal rule of good writing was never write a story on the theme of false teeth. He thought this was absurd. Hence he wrote not one story about false teeth but two! And both are bizarre.

"A Visit to the Dentist" appears in *Among the Dahlias* (1957) and "The Biter Bit" appears in *The Marmalade Bird* (1973). The sixteen-year lapse in time between these stories reveals much about Sansom's tenacity or perversity!

"A Visit to the Dentist" is the story of a middle-aged man named Pemberton who leaves his dentist's office with a new bridge of plastic teeth. He is still partly drugged as he wanders into an expensive-looking, dimly lit restaurant for coffee. As he muddles through the gory events that have just transpired in the dentist's office, he realizes with horror that he has one particularly strong dislike—objects made from plastic.

He noticed that the brown brittle electric light sockets soon split, he had broken his fingernails trying to open a plastic-sealed medicine carton, somebody had once sent him a set of occasional cups and saucers whose very touch and unusual lightness had inspired something near to horror in him. And now, he reflected, as he sat in this strange restaurant, he had a plastic device in his mouth for life. . . .[25]

He offends the waitress, upsets a stand of cakes, and hears himself whistle out rather than speak words. In his muddled, drugged state he mistakes a customer's poodle for a cat and calls it nice pussy. (Sansom can never resist the double meaning of pussy!)

As the drug starts to wear off, he sees that the restaurant appears to have many stylish women in it, all with poodles. As a burly male customer accuses Pemberton of insulting his lady friend, Pemberton tries to explain that he is not drunk. A humorous exchange occurs as the big man says, "Well, I can rumble your type all right," and Pemberton, misunderstanding, says, "Rumble? This is all Greek to me. . . . And I haven't my Liddell and Scott handy."

The man angrily asks if Pemberton is being funny, obviously not understanding that Liddell and Scott is a reference book. To make matters worse, Pemberton snatches for another reference book that may be more familiar and says, "Well, let's say my Baedeker."[27]

This sends the place into an uproar as his words are construed as his wanting to go to bed with the woman escorted by the big man. A fight ensues, Pemberton is punched in the mouth, and the new bridge breaks. With blood in his mouth, he hails a cab to return the broken denture to the dentist before closing time.

This story dwells on the embarrassment occasioned by the dentures, the pain at the dentist's office, and difficulty of a middle-aged man in adjusting to a new way of speaking and viewing himself. In contrast, "The Biter Bit" dwells on the acceptance of dentures by an older man and a practical joke played on him by two young men.

"The Biter Bit" is an extended anecdote about a young man, Thomas John, who likes to visit joke shops specializing in "grotesque masks, greenish gloves in the form of terrible claws, giant-toed false feet to slip over your shoes, bandaged fingers running with blood, even stick-on 'pus-topped' boils . . . itching powder, stink-bombs . . . carefully curled brown snakes of 'Naughty Doggie' dirt . . . tell-tale cat-sick, and a pneumatically controlled plate-wobbler."[28]

When Thomas John and Ted are told a story by old Paddy, who is really only fifty, about taking out his dentures in mid-ocean and tossing them into the water but catching them before they fell, they spur him to reenact the trick over a nearby river. As is expected, Paddy takes out the dentures, tosses them toward the river, and fails to catch them in time. They see the dentures float away and sink. No search can bring them back.

So Thomas John goes to the joke shop and buys an upper set of false teeth. The boys contrive to take Paddy fishing, and while he dozes they tie the dentures to his line. When he awakens he is delighted to discover the dentures. Mud and all, he pops them into his mouth and declares that they fit better than ever!

Thomas John proves to be a poor loser because Paddy's naive delight in the teeth makes him feel ashamed. This shame and the

ensuing irritation Thomas develops toward Paddy, even after he has
confessed the trick, is not convincing. How much more interesting
this story would have been had Sansom examined the character of a
practical joker rather than pad it with lists of joke-shop items and the
history of dentures! He should have heeded Chekhov's answer to his
publisher, Souvorin. Souvorin criticized a story about horse thieves,
called "The Devils," for its detached point of view of the characters
and their problems. Chekhov defended himself in this way:

You scold me for objectivity, calling it indifference to good and evil, the
absence of ideas and ideals. . . . When I depict horse thieves you would like
me to say: the stealing of horses is bad. But surely this has long since been
known without my saying it. . . . My business is to show them as they are. I
write: You are dealing with horse thieves—then you should know that they
are not beggars but well-fed people, that they belong to a cult, and that horse
stealing with them is not just theft but a passion. Of course, it would be
pleasant to combine art with preaching, but for me personally this is
extremely difficult, and almost impossible because of technical considera-
tions. Clearly, in order to portray horse thieves in seven hundred lines, I must
all the time speak and think as they would, and feel with their feelings;
otherwise, if I introduce subjective notes, the characters will become
indistinct and the story not as compact as all short stories ought to be.[29]

Chekhov's words apply to a practical joker such as Thomas. How and
why he is one is far more interesting than his guilt about being one.
Sansom fails in telling *how* a joker thinks and feels.

After reading these two stories on dentures, I conclude that the
brochure that warned against trying to write an interesting story
about false teeth was right! Although Pemberton is a more interesting
man than Thomas John, both men are manipulated into situations
for the sake of a pun rather than insight into character. Sansom
should have declined the challenge of the brochure!

VII   *Later Stories on Societal Themes*

Although Sansom tried to write of the effects of the Welfare State
and middle-class affluence in his few novels (*The Last Hours of
Sandra Lee*, *Goodbye*, and *A Young Wife's Tale*), he never felt
comfortable with the results. However, in the last eight years of his
life, he successfully depicts the problems of contemporary life in
several short stories. In *The Marmalade Bird*, his last collection, there
are four such stories.

The first story "Down at the Hydro," depicts the flirtation of an elderly colonel with a married woman at an expensive dieters' resort. Lying in their gazebos, starving on salads, enduring sitz baths and massages, and, above all, experiencing rejuvenation, the characters and their fellow dieters feel justified in expending a great deal of money for someone else to discipline them into thinness. In addition, the dieters are treated to lectures on the efficacy of mineral waters and enemas.

Sansom catches not only the tone of the Hydro but also the attitude of "patients" with the gentle comic spirit of Bunin.

It had set a pace of some intimacy. No one would go so far as to say they were all one big family, nor did the staff say so. There was surprisingly little archness in the attitude of the staff. Someone indeed had labelled the huts "gazebos," but mostly because once there had been a old gazebo thereabouts. And there was a habit of likening patients to their cars: "Your engine's clogged and tired—isn't it just natural to come in for a decoking?" But this was, after all, perhaps the easiest way to get at the average contemporary mind. Though the allusion sometimes misfired, as indeed with Deirdre Mackay herself, who had been caught out with a petit beurre one morning. Without preamble, the nurse had said: "Somebody's taking their car out of the garage too soon!"[30]

The analogy of humans to cars demonstrates the theme of a flaccid society that has sacrificed its humanity for the efficiency of technology. The members of this society willingly allow themselves to be victimized by the image-builders of the business world in preference to exerting free will and determining their own condition.

The second story "Mamma Mia," is a brief sexual encounter between a young Italian migratory worker and a middle-aged working-class widow. This story demonstrates the sexual permissiveness of the age better than *A Young Wife's Tale* because Sansom is telling the story objectively without intruding his usual moral judgment.

When the widow, Mrs. Brown, becomes pregnant, she becomes the object of jokes about immaculate conception. But she ignores them and ". . . as jokes will create truth, there were some who even began to believe it: the old girl looked so queenly, almost holy with her little dark-eyed babe beside her."[31]

She never attempts to find Piero and he, for his part, retains the mellow memory of a warm, giving woman who illustrated the loveliness of English women. Thus Sansom handles not only illicit sex but illegitimate children with a light touch in keeping with contemporary society's less condemnatory views.

The third story "A Day Out," is a breathless account of a cockney family's outing in their car. The roads are crowded with other affluent workers, roadside restaurants, and signs. The son of the family, who is the narrator, gets particular pleasure out of stopping in the men's room to pull off and on his new nonwool synthetic shirt and watch the sparks fly. He and his siblings drink many Cokes on their bumper-to-bumper excursion and voice continual amazement at the new sights in the amusement park, the new supermarket, and the new merchandise. Near the end of the jolly outing, his mother tells him to pull over to the side so his father can throw up and not dirty the car.

For a brief moment, the narrator looks up at the stars, his first glance at something that is not man-made. He thinks,

> ... The whole sky's soft like velvet and d'you know, even with all them other cars passing, when I look up at that sky it all feels dead quiet. Up there, I think, it's going on for ever ... silver stars like pepper dust going on forever and ever and ever ... and I feel so lonely I want to cry ... it's so bleeding beautiful like.... Still we don't want to go on about *that* sort of thing.... Did the whole sixty-one miles in under five hours ... a right good day had by all.[32]

Through the clichés of this young man's vocabulary Sansom implies a great deal. The new rich enjoy their material possessions with the gusto that the advertising world advocates. The price they will pay cannot be reckoned, but the meaningless conversations of the family forebode a disintegration of meaningful relationships of man to man and man to nature.

The fourth story "The Day the Lift ... ," describes the entrapment of a prosperous businessman, A. B. Bowlsend, in an elevator. Before he enters the elevator, he is reviewing in his mind the blessings of suburban life and his family of a wife and two daughters. After he finds himself trapped in the elevator with a strange man who does not panic, Bowlsend becomes hysterical. He screams and attracts the attention of Healey, the man he has come to do business with.

Once rescued, Bowlsend is mortified when Healey asks where the woman is who screamed. He is upset that Healey only offers him a glass of water and treats the matter lightly. Finding it hard to admit that he was only in the elevator a quarter of an hour, he rewards himself by stopping on the way home at a pub for a large brandy.

Once home, he does an about-face on family plans. He tells them,

... We are *not* going to the Wapham marina. Waste of time and money. It's time we all stiffened up a bit. Ought to be thankful we're alive, not spend the time always wanting more of this, more of that. And you Marlene [his teenage daughter], you're to be back home at eleven o'clock tonight. And every night, see?[33]

While Bowlsend is comical in his posturing, his experience conveys Sansom's message well. Prosperity must be used in conjunction with the Puritan ethic of discipline; otherwise man will be incapable of surviving the vicissitudes of life.

VIII *Sansom's Two Favorite Stories*

"Life, Death," originally published in *Lord Love Us* in 1954 and in *The Stories of William Sansom* in 1954, and "The Bonfire," published in *The Marmalade Bird* in 1973, are two favorite stories of Sansom's. They are interesting to examine because they were written at the beginning and end of his career. Also, they handle the subject of death in a masterful prose style.

"Life, Death" is a simple story told as if it were a ballad. A fishmonger falls in love with a shy customer, woos her, weds her, and eventually loses her and their baby to death. He tells his story in the first person. From his enthusiastic outpouring of words, he creates a happy picture of an artist-fishmonger's work. For example,

Now I had my white coat and my blue apron, and how I'd jam my straw on pleased to greet the trade. But first I finish off—now I'd got my central. Mackerel, trouts and my red-spotted plaice-lings—those coloured fellows I would take next. Striped mackerels I'd make into a ring, and place a crab within. Two rings I'd make, one each side to balance. Then stars of rainbow trout, all wet colours one each side to balance. Then stars of rainbow trout, all wet colours of the rainbow dew. But my plaice—my good brown plaice with the bright red dabs, these I'd bend tail to head, tail to head so they'd make a round, and I'd set them plumb in the middle below the big turbot, for a braver-marked fish would be hard to find.[34]

This arrangement of fish is a piece of conceptual art that awakens Sansom's sensibilities. Michel-Michot likens the fantasy and creativity of the fishmonger at work to Sansom at work: "He plays with words just as the boy plays with fish, following the inward pressure of the moment, arranging them so as to create beauty and delight. And Sansom's gift for revivifying worn-out expressions, clichés, or traditional 'poetic' diction by introducing common-speech phrases is similar to the boy's beauty-making power."[35]

Once the fish-monger falls in love, even his fellow workers seem beautiful.

So I was happier than for all time past. In my straw in the sun, tiles around, my good slab iced, my slab with water-spray and fern: red buses passing huge out front, and people always passing too—all busy passing in the sun, and a smile from me with my straw cocked and my heart-a-wing. Even Milly got a smile, I could smile for dark Milly. She sat in her cash all day, dark like a spider-crab taking the flies off fish and giving them again for pennies and silver: or like a foreign god she was, one with six arms, taking offerings in her fat hole and chinking wealth and prayer all day, or the night that was day for *her*. But I gave her a smile. And old Jim-at-the-Back thought I was crazed with my digs and my whistles. I heard him chuckle over his sluice of slice and gut out back.[36]

The use of *so* and *and* sustain the ballad style and give the passage simple, childlike phrasing. Nevertheless, the colors of sun and red buses, the sound of coins in the cash box, the odor of water and fish convey the complex ways in which the boy's view of his world is mellowing.

The ending, after the loss of his wife and daughter, resembles the traditional lament of ballads.

They've gone, I said, my loved ones are gone. Please only give me back my slab—and they, who knew, did that. But I tell you this, my slab never is the same again, there's a shade about for me.[37]

The boy has become a man. He has risen to be manager of the fish store in order to provide a good life for his family. Once he loses them, he yearns for the comfort of his old clerking job at the slab, for his ambition has died. Like the traditional lament, the story ends with his altered condition in life and his need to talk forever about his terrible loss.

"The Bonfire" was placed by Sansom significantly at the end of his last collection, *The Marmalade Bird*. He regarded it as one of his best pieces of writing, particularly in its ending.[38] Suprisingly, "The Bonfire" returns to the subject of fire with its dangerous entrapment. Sansom proves he has not exhausted this subject. The protagonist, however, differs from the protagonist of the fireman stories in his advanced age and house-proud attitude. But Wilkins, the protagonist, is just as conscientious as Fireman Flower.

The story begins with the wife, Mrs. Wilkins, looking at her husband's bruised knees and asking him what gigantic secretary has been sitting on them lately. Wilkins looks at his bruised knees and wonders if wishing to have his new typist sit on them actually caused telepathic bruises; he replies that all he has been doing is breaking sticks for a bonfire at the end of the garden.

He prides himself on making a fire by the boy-scout method, which makes him feel as if he has mastered the elements. But his wife is upset by the bruises this method causes and she says, "That garden'll be the death of you. . . . Last week lumbago, now bruises. All those scratches from the roses. Poets have died from the prick of a thorn."[39]

Her prognostication almost comes true. As Wilkins walks to the end of his garden, Sansom reverses the familiar design of a realistic rendering of the scene. The man is passive; "things" become active. Against the end-wall lies the blackened bonfire patch with its wild mysteriousness.

He . . . felt it to be some sort of sacred grove. It was darkly shadowed by neighbouring trees, which also let through curiously bright shafts of sunshine like occasional beams of sunlight in a church . . . and gave the whole quietly sleeping place a pagan, holy look. But sleeping? It rather seemed to be waiting, watching. "It'll be the death of you," echoed back to him as he felt once again the quiet threat of so much darkly green growth, and he threw down his boxes and paper almost like a challenge. "Just try," he told the poisoned nettles. Each nettle grew exactly upright, its pointed leaves arrowed downwards, intense with held action.[40]

Then suddenly his prayers are answered. A gust of wind blows the flame out. No sooner does this happen than Wilkins scoffs at his foolishness about calling the grove sacred. As if a higher force reads his mind, a small rim of red sparks begins to eat away at the sheet of newspaper.

With practicality he decides to remove his trousers and rid himself of the thorns that are pinioning him. But the trouser legs are too tight-fitting to remove easily. He stands up, fly unzipped, trouser tops flapping above the knee, feeling absurd. As the flame burns secretly like a magic curse, he feels helpless as a child. He hears an ominous crackling and Sansom describes its effect with a crescendo worthy of Proust.

A smell sweet as childhood rose up to Wilkins' nose, the remembered smell of paper and kindling sticks from a fire grate. Wee Willie Wilkin, child, boy, youth and now large strong provident man held fast in a trap built by himself, built with care of dry things and air for the maximum efficient flame, topped by a climber dug up with equal care for a more efficient flowering of garden, yet now a thick-tentacled dry octopus reaching out to grip and hold him.[41]

His indignation at the realization that he has carefully entrapped himself causes him to gain extraordinary strength. He frees one leg to kick the fire out but the other leg is still pinned by thorns and his trousers which are halfway down his legs.

He is still in danger of burning to death. The heat hits him and he finally cries weakly for help. The fire hits his face and body. His body convulses and he wrenches himself free, dragging the rose with him. He rolls about on the lawn in his smoldering clothes and collapses.

His wife comes to the rescue with a wheelbarrow which she uses to drag him away from the fire. The last two lines of the story, which Sansom said "wrote themselves," are:

Then she stood quite still, a figure of sudden peace, and quietly watered her husband.

And the bonfire burned on, not so high now, but settling down to eat up all the year's succession of events, the winter's storm-broken branches, brown ferns and greyed chrysanthemums, the dried daffodils of spring, early irises, prunings, a large reaping of weeds, the first dead roses of summer.[42]

The husband blends into the landscape that he formerly thought he was master of. The wife waters him as she would a smoldering object. The visual effects of this scene are superb.

So is the last touch of the first dead roses of summer. The scent is pervasive. Roses suggest serenity, a symbol of the Virgin Mary. They also suggest perfection, which is what Wilkins aspires to in his garden. Paradoxically, the roses have thorns which not only actively subjugate this house-proud man but also nearly cause him to lose his life.

In this last published short story of Sansom's, he reveals both his early interests and those that came later. His early interests centered around the natural element of fire and the way in which it disabused a character of his notion of reality. His later interests centered around human adjustment to the vicissitudes of life.

One of his ardent critics, John Vickery, has made comments on early stories that are applicable to "The Bonfire." In "William Sansom and Logical Empiricism" Vickery says,

... [We] find the questions of Sansom's characters are those of purpose or cause, essence, properties, those, in short, asked by the metaphysician. ... So Sansom shows how the topics, questions, and unknown answers [irritate his mind and force him to rely on unknowns]. ... .[43]

Sansom's characters learn that they cannot eliminate ambiguity. They must learn to live with frustrations and their own mediocrities. But to a degree, as in Wilkins's finding superhuman strength to wrench himself free of the fire, they can control their lives. A neosurrealist work results from this juxtaposition of the commonplace with the horrific. The resolution between the ideals of Wilkins and his reaction to nightmare forces is a matter of equilibrium which Sansom creates in this story in a masterly fashion.

IX *Summary of the Short Stories*

Throughout his thirty years of writing, Sansom gathered strength in the short-story form. His first stories were brief, epigrammatic, and moved quickly. They were in harmony with the nervous, fragmented life of the 1940s. Reflecting the influence of Poe and Grandville, these stories dwelled on the bizarre with no irrelevancies or digressions. His use of language to emphasize mood was right from the start lyrical and polished.

During the second decade of his writing career, his short stories began to sparkle with wit and irony. They also became less surrealistic and more romantic. The resolutions of the plots, when the stories were plotted and not sketches or slices of life, were neither comic nor tragic. The protagonist was allowed a certain freedom of action but not the kind of freedom that permits him to control his destiny or integrate himself back into society. Reflecting the influence of Proust, these stories dwelled on explicit details of setting that subtly defined character. Like Proust, Sansom evoked the feelings of déjà vu with his ability to make the reader abruptly conscious of past sensations. Thus, he captured the mystery in the relationship between the sexes as he was rarely able to do in his novels. At times his stories reflect the influence of Bunin in their simple factual framework containing less explicit detail but letting feelings speak for themselves. Images solidify and move of their own motion. The themes pertain less to illusion and reality and more to the necromancy of love, time, and death.

During the last decade of his writing career, his short stories reflected the angst of contemporary life and his own mature view of the human condition. So versatile was he by the end of his life that he could call upon the bizarre effects of his early stories, the witty and romantic effects of his later stories, and the wisdom of his middle age to write a variety of stories. The vigor and sophistication of his last stories are entirely consistent with the excellence of all his previous stories, proving Elizabeth Bowen's description of him as "a short-storyist par excellence, a short-storyist by birth, addiction and destiny."

CHAPTER 6

Miscellaneous Works
and Conclusion

THROUGHOUT his years as a writer, Sansom has often written commentary to richly illustrated books of photographs or drawings, and, in two instances, he has even done line drawings himself. Some of the illustrated books for which he has written commentary are *Westminster in War* (1947); *Christmas* (1968); *The Birth of a Story* (1972); *Proust and His World* (1973); *Victorian Life in Photos* (1974); and *Grandville* (1975). At the time of his death he was working on an introduction to a collection of the short stories of Ivan Bunin.

Besides writing three children's books, *The Light That Went Out* (1953), *It Was Really Charlie's Castle* (1953), and *Skimpy* (1974), Sansom wrote and illustrated *The Get-Well Colouring Book* in 1963 and illustrated *Who's Zoo* by Michael Brande in 1963. In addition to the aforementioned volumes, there are many essays published in commercial magazines over the past thirty years.

Of particular interest are *The Birth of a Story* and *Proust and His World*. Each reveals his working methods, goals, and taste.

I The Birth of a Story

The Birth of a Story contains an essay on his aesthetic philosophy; a story called "No Smoking in the Apron," which was collected in the volume *The Ulcerated Milkman* (1966): an explanation of how the story was written; the manuscript, with marginal notes of explanation of revisions; the typescript; and an epilogue.

While the plot of "No Smoking in the Apron" is fabricated, the characters, Duncan or Dunko and Mrs. Cabot, do not seem to be. They are passengers on a flight from Copenhagen to London but do not meet until they are walking on the apron of the Copenhagen airport. Dunko decides to empty his fountain pen and the ink, whipped by a sudden gust, flies onto the woman's white dress. She is in the process of applying lipstick and becomes so angry at Dunko that she stabs his shirt and suit with her lipstick.

In the airplane Dunko tries to make amends. Mrs. Cabot acts seductively and tells him how dissatisfied she is with the vacation she has just had. They then share food and talk. A storm cements their relationship when she huddles in his arms out of fear.

As Dunko worries about the cost of replacing the dress that his pen has ruined, a sensuality takes over their mood. He learns that the dress cost very little and he is delighted to find her available after the plane lands. They go to a hotel and make love for the rest of the afternoon. When they part, they exchange cards, as in a duel. But there is no duel, just a final goodbye.

She leaves to catch her train to the country. He returns home to his wife who kisses and kisses him so enthusiastically that, ironically, she believes it is her lipstick on his shirt and suit. This kind of humorous twist to the end of their sad compulsion to make love is typically Sansomian.

In his explanation of how the story was born, he tells of being intrigued by the setting of an airplane and a chance meeting between a man and a woman. But the idea did not jell until one day when he was cleaning his fountain pen while standing near the door to his garden. A sudden breeze blew a blob of ink dangerously near his white trousers. Instantly, a woman's white dress, spoiled, flew into his mind, and his plot was formed.

He chose the surname Duncan because it suggested to him a solid presence. Yet he uses his Christian nickname, Dunko, to be intimate from the start. He chose Copenhagen as the place to begin because its airport photographed well in his memory. But the title, "No Smoking in the Apron," was taken from a phrase posted at the London airport. What he writes about it is revealing:

. . . I found [this phrase] . . . both striking and funny (in the loose sense that anything to do with kippers, sausages, aprons is in England traditionally a sign for broad humour) and it also had a brooding sense of guilt about it. This matched the two brooding senses of danger, of air flight itself and of the conflict of the protagonists, which should threaten throughout the story.[1]

All these decisions he made quickly. But when the episode of the flying ink came up, his unconscious took over. While more travelers seemed fearful, her heavy makeup seemed to give her a carapace, "proof against anything or anyone." That the red lipstick which happened to be in her hand when the ink landed on her dress was luck. ". . . [It] took a large place in the whole story. It also served as part of a kind of classic symbol, in the way an architectural facade can employ classical motifs for stability and secure acceptance—there the red, white and blue of the national flag."[2]

The exchange of cards underlined the absurd theatricality of the scene. The experience of the storm cemented their relationship by touch. Mrs. Cabot has turned temptress and Sansom, the moralist, writes:

. . . As Dunko allows himself to be tempted, his guilt (and one hopes, the reader's) is put into big booming capital letters by the fatal sign, ominous, vaguely ridiculous, NO SMOKING ON THE APRON."[3]

Perhaps the lack of guilt over adultery, so prevalent in modern society, is a weakness. Nevertheless, Sansom is being here too intrusive. It is one thing to make a character feel guilty. But it is quite a different thing to assume the reader will feel such deep empathy with a guilt-ridden character.

On the other hand, what Sansom writes about the hotel room at sunset, which was actually a room he knew in childhood, affects the readers' sensibilities. The memory sounds as if it were filtered through Proust's mind.

A rather badly . . . furnished room in some seaside resort [it resembled]. . . . The dressing-table was of varnished yellow wood. The bay window where it stood was not curved but sharp-cornered in a triptych shape. Perhaps . . . I myself had some strong emotional experience in a room which reminded me of the childhood room? . . . It is all forgotten, yet very clear in geography and essence.

And it is coupled with another memory from my childhood, with the fact that the dying sunlight on the wall, the dead gold, comes from the time when I . . . spent weeks in one room recovering from scarlet fever. It was a west-facing room, I grew intimately to know the sadness of evening sunlight and I have never forgotten it.[4]

He sees the coda of the guilty Dunko, still smudged with lipstick, being kissed by his wife as no trick ending. He establishes two important matters: the loving trust of the wife and the finality of his infidelity. This produces the happy-sad ending he and other writers strive for in imitation of life going on after the last word of the story.

Reviewers differed in their opinion of the *Birth of a Story*. John
Brinner, in the *Teacher*, doubts if the book had to be written and finds
it poorly proofread.[5] The *Times Literary Supplement*, however, says,
". . . He is particularly good . . . on the vital job of the 'chisel'—
learnt, it is clear, from the ruthless job of pruning advertising copy,
and demonstrated a dozen times."[6]

II Proust and His World

Published in 1973, this book contains many pictures, drawings,
and photographs along with Sansom's text. He has imaginatively
coordinated moments in Proust's life with pictures of Parisian life.

The thematic framework of *Proust and His World* is our collective
memory of a golden past. "Thus, we are all walking computers
carrying about the records of past angles of light, sounds, tastes,
which, when by chance brought to our notice again, provoke a most
mysterious and satisfying thrill: momentarily we are outside time."[7]
From this statement it is evident why Sansom is interested in Proust.
They share contemplation of past events through the senses.

The book, on the whole, was well received. A few critics felt
Sansom shrouded Proust in pretension and used odd phrases such as
"etiolated mud."[8] But even so, they commended Sansom on his
energetic and vivid writing style.

III *Conclusion*

No sensible judgment of William Sansom's writing can be either
wholly favorable or wholly unfavorable. Of the nine novels he wrote,
only three (*The Body, The Loving Eye, The Cautious Heart*) are
outstanding and one (*Goodbye*) is very good. Almost all of his short
stories are excellent. Nevertheless, everything he wrote is character-
ized by some individual weaknesses as well as strengths.

On the negative side, Sansom's deficiencies can be epitomized. His
love of the surface of physical life sometimes carries him away, as in
scenic details of *A Bed of Roses* or *A Young Wife's Tale*. His prose
decoration can overemphasize setting to the detriment of character,
plot, or theme. He may invest too much space on dull characters such
as Hans Feet (*Hans Feet in Love*) or Sandra and her co-workers (*The
Last Hours of Sandra Lee*), and his clever manipulation of words
may fail to animate.

Another fault to which Sansom is prone is contrivance. Thoughts may gush from his characters' minds without artistic control when he wants to be humorous, as in *Hans Feet in Love, Goodbye,* or *The Last Hours of Sandra Lee.* The joke or pun may overwhelm a scene rather than serve as a means to build tension or further insight into a character. Even in an excellent novel, such as *The Loving Eye,* the comic relief supplied by Leslie sometimes borders on bad taste. This fault, however, occurs in novels and not in short stories probably because the smaller space of short works encourages an ecomony of words and balance of tension with comic relief.

Besides contrivance for comic effect, Sansom often contrives his endings. Many of his romantic protagonists end their life on the page by living happily ever after (Henry Bishop in *The Body,* Louise in *A Bed of Roses,* Eve in *The Face of Innocence,* and Matthew in *The Loving Eye*), even though most of their obsessions and machinations imply lifelong personality problems. Not until the last decade of his life did Sansom seem to square these romantic ideas with reality. When he did, his endings became more neutral—as in *A Young Wife's Tale* and the stories in his last collection, *The Marmalade Bird*—and thus more realistic.

Still another fault is Sansom's substitution of moral seriousness for plot. While he stopped outright moralizing in the endings of short stories written after *Fireman Flower,* he often laced his novels with disapproval of sexual freedom. The infidelity of Julie and Eve, teasing of Sandra Lee, and dreams of casual sex of Hans Feet may have shocked prewar readers, when Sansom was a boy. But, today most readers feel little compassion for characters with such dilemmas. Sansom lacks the ability of Iris Murdoch to create complex characters by combining myth with intellectual discussion and bedroom farce; Sansom's sexual scenes are more one-liners than sustained fantasies. Failing the ability to flavor the sexual scenes with Murdoch's artfulness, he might have succeeded in making these scenes more dramatic if they were generated by the strong religious credo of, for example, Graham Greene. Since these scenes are prompted by neither artfulness nor dogma, Sansom's attitude toward sexual immorality appears to be anachronistic.

When he substitutes other aspects of moral seriousness than the sexual for plot, as in *The Face of Innocence* and *A Bed of Roses,* in which the impetus for action comes from two psychopathic personalities, he appears to have written case studies rather than fiction. In contrast, Joyce Cary could transmute a narcissistic artist or minister into a heroic force in his fictional world. In a 1955 review of *The Passionate North, Something Terrible, Something Lovely,* and *A Bed of Roses,* Howard Nemerov admired the literate and serious aspects of the novel *A Bed of Roses* but still experienced a central feeling of disappointment in his response to the work. However, he noted that Sansom's two collections of short stories did not evoke this disappointment.[9] Nemerov was undoubtedly alluding to Sansom's moralistic intrusions in some longer works as opposed to his objectivity in shorter works.

Sansom's general success in a novel or short story depends on whether he can integrate his characters into the setting and make them credible. The jealousy of Henry Bishop, the yearning of Matthew Ligne, and the exasperation of the pianist-narrator of *The Cautious Heart* are as vivid as the sense of la vie manquée with which Henry James embues his narrators. Sansom vivifies his male characters by his impressionistic technique. In fact, their obsessions define the plot. However, he has failed to create women protagonists as well. Louise, in *A Bed of Roses,* Eve, in *The Face of Innocence,* Madge, in *The Body,* and Marie, in *The Cautious Heart,* lack the dimension and depth that would render them more interesting. Consequently he is prone in weaker novels to rely more heavily on plot than on character. Yet, even in a weak novel such as *The Last Hours of Sandra Lee,* his poetic style works its magic. Anthony Burgess says of that novel, ". . . Poetry is conjured out of the very paper-clips in a London office and the cadences of speech continue to be wonderfully caught. . . . The heroine delights with what she looks like, not with what she is; she is a triumph of the cosmetician's art, a lay-figure and not a human being."[10]

Just as Sansom's defects are evident, so too are his virtues. First of all, his love of the surface of physical life—a fire, a woman at a window, the feet of diners seen from under a table, or the regimen of a dieters' resort—leads us from a self-tortured mind to a kind of philosophy. His characters try to cope with a world that is increasingly mystifying and alarming. At his best, Sansom raises the comman man's absurdities to the level of universal anxieties. The thematic preoccupation with loneliness, its pathos, and punishment empower his stories as parables. While C. P. Snow, Anthony Powell, and Joyce Cary wrote massive serials examining psychological reality through social history and Lawrence Durrell in his *Alexandrian Quartet* explored point of view through time and space, Sansom preferred to remain on the surface of his fiction. Yet, by doing so, he was able to achieve the contrary effect of delving into the human spirit. Of this artfulness John Vickery says,

. . . [Sansom's] outlook more nearly resembles that of the contemporary empiricist and *analytic* philosophers of Oxford and Cambridge (particularly striking since he is a non-university man) than that of the older continental rationalist or today's existentialist.[11]

Thus to many critics Sansom's fiction is primarily philosophical involving passive protagonists struggling with themselves. Of his contemporaries, the writers whose works might best be contrasted with Sansom's are "the angries." The angry young men, Kingsley Amis, John Braine, John Wain, and later on, Alan Sillitoe wrote social protest novels involving activist protagonists struggling with the British Establishment of the 1950s. Coming from lower-class or lower-middle-class backgrounds, they raised themselves above their class chiefly through education. Amis's novel *Lucky Jim* revels in the antics of Jim, a clever toady who teaches medieval history in academia. Jim is socially displaced and reverts to his own lowbrow tastes: jazz, television, science fiction, and drinking beer in pubs. Sansom, on the other hand, came from an upper-middle-class background and *chose* not to go to the university. This choice and his choice to quit banking were his only two "rebellions" against his parents, who served as the Establishment to him. He never rebelled against the privileges of class, but he did, as he aged, grow more and more fascinated by the very culture that the angry young men emerged from—the lower middle class. He found beauty in the accents, diction, and values of that class and lovingly integrated them into the bulk of his work, as may be found in the neighbors of Henry Bishop, in *The Body*, the neighbors of Tony Lyle, in *The Loving Eye*, the neighbors in *Goodbye*, and most of the main characters in the short stories of *The Marmalade Bird*.

Another strength of Sansom's is his ability to create atmosphere with unusual, well-chosen words and imaginative effects called Kafkaesque, but, as I have proved, really Poe-like. Two other writers active in the 1950s, Rex Warner and Anthony Burgess, shared with Sansom this ability to create in their early works a bizarre atmosphere that engulfed the innocent protagonist. However, the protagonists of Warner and Burgess were concerned with man's avarice and the dystopian world of the future, while Fireman Flower and Henry Bishop, for example, were chiefly concerned with themselves. It is

interesting to note that Burgess himself writes, ". . . The posture of
Kafka disciple does not last for long with any of our writers who first
made their names with nightmare."[12] This statement certainly applies
to Sansom, whose later works were less nightmarish. Nevertheless, he
always retained his talent for swiftly invoking eeriness in atmosphere.

One of the most recurrent themes in Sansom's fiction that he
depicts particularly well is the contemporary theme of the willing
victim in search of his/her victimizer. To Sansom the worst threat to
the individual is human violence. This theme can be found in the
fiction of William Golding and Muriel Spark. Golding and Spark,
however, differ from Sansom in their handling of this theme. Golding
focuses on the evil inherent in man (*The Lord of the Flies, Pincher
Martin*) in fabulistic language. His characters are rarely full blooded
because they represent a *roman a thèse*. Muriel Spark, who is also
interested in evil, fleshes out her character-victims (*The Driver's Seat*
and *The Abbess of Crewe*) with satirical language. Sansom does
neither because he is not interested in theological concepts of evil nor
societal concepts of evil. Rather, he focuses on the devious ways in
which man's perception of himself affects his environment, works to
destroy him, but ultimately saves him. Such memorable short-story
characters as Doole ("Among the Dahlias"), Clara ("Various Temptations"), Wilkins ("The Bonfire"), and Tressiter ("To the Rescue!")
illustrate Sansom's portrayal of victims by synthesizing individual
problems to reach a universal meaning.

Another writer concerned with evil whose name has been linked
with Sansom's is Angus Wilson. Wilson's novel *Hemlock and After*,
published in 1952, created a sensation by its open recognition of
homosexuality and depiction of the inadequacy of liberal values in
the face of evil. But, since Sansom is less interested in evil than in the
individual's perception of reality, his work cannot be compared easily
with Wilson's, at least not his novels. However, many of Sansom's
short stories ("A World of Glass," "Episode at Gastein," "Life,
Death") do compare with Wilson's novels in their emphasis on the
disintegration of a man or a way of life into chaos even though they
attempt at the very end of the work to restore order.

Sansom's greatest strength is his style. He possesses an innate
ability to reproduce light and shadow, sounds, speech rhythms, and
attitudes of lower-middle-class English men and women. He views his
scenes and characters with such clarity of language that he enables
readers to see and hear as few writers do. Why this ability is more

evident in his short stories than in his novels is due to the limited boundaries of the short story as opposed to the elaborate patterning of the novel. In a short story, Sansom is neither leisurely nor discursive; rather he relies on the lessons he has learned from Poe. He selects and compresses a single subject at "white heat," maintaining tension at all times. Where the novel may sometimes tempt him to prolong a scene or portray yet another facet of a character's personality, the short story does not. Both Sansom and Elizabeth Bowen capture the moment by resonating it through setting and character. For example, Bowen resonates the moment the cat jumps or the demon lover calls for his betrothed and Sansom resonates the moment when the woman screams in the quarry or the man's trousers catch fire from the present to the past to the future. Happily for Sansom, resonating the moment does not involve plotting out the story, which can be troublesome for him.

In addition, the short story as a form seems more compatible with the fragmented nature of contemporary life and relationships. As human life becomes more precarious, writers such as Sansom grapple with one major issue at a time in a particular piece of work. What raises his short stories to the realm of art that Henry James called "blest," "shapely," and "beautiful" is Sansom's polished prose. Whether he is describing bizarre, allegorical, or everyday events, his crafted statements are always lyrical. His best stories, such as "Life, Death," "Fireman Flower," and "The Bonfire," are tone poems that sustain the inner harmonies of character with the outer dissonances of setting; the surface and texture of his prose become his vision. Because he shares this interest in craft with the novelist Henry Green, who was active in the late 1940s and 1950s, the two men's works have been frequently linked together. Both were experimental, during those years, in their emphasis on technique. The titles of Green's novels (*Blindness, Living, Loving, Back, Concluding*) reveal something of his characters' worlds. They have no real plans and let things happen to them. In contrast, Sansom's characters are obsessed by a body, a woman at the window, and a face of innocence so that they are driven to unearth their illusions in order to come to terms with reality. Green writes in short, elliptical sentences while Sansom writes in elaborate, lyrical sentences. Nevertheless, the two writers are linked. I conclude that the linkage is due to their interest in the aesthetics of style rather than in the moral or psychological preoccupations of their contemporaries.

Despite Sansom's participation in the postwar literary world, he remained a maverick. After 1945, when the novel reasserted its realistic potential for moral and social concerns, Sansom was writing in a surrealist vein. By the 1960s, the hopes for a revival of realism began to disintegrate. The mood changed and many of the novelists, such as Doris Lessing, Iris Murdoch, Anthony Burgess, and Angus Wilson, began to change with it. As Malcolm Bradbury says, ". . . Constituents of the modernist impulse, especially its tendency toward play and game, its stress on art as forgery, and its surreal and fabulous dimension, began to appear significant again. . . . The idea of the novel as realistic tale was challenged."[13] But it was not challenged by Sansom. Instead, he withdrew from his original efforts at experimentalism and became more realistic. These shortcomings should not influence a final assessment of his achievements. Perhaps his value is like the value Evelyn Waugh predicts for his contemporaries:

> It may happen in the next hundred years that the English novelists of the present day will come to be valued as we now value the arts and craftsmen of the late eighteenth century. The originators, the exuberant men, are extinct and in their place subsists and modestly flourishes a generation notable for elegance and variety of contrivance.[14]

In the last year of his life, Sansom wrote introductions to two books: one on Grandville and his illustrations and the other on the collected short stories of Ivan Bunin. These introductions bring his interests in surrealism and humor full circle. Beginning with the moment of epiphany that Sansom experienced when his friend and mentor, Norman Cameron, took him to see his first surrealist show, Sansom learned how to create the special reality of an individual. Ending with the comic range that he developed mainly through his close study of Bunin's work, his last short story, "The Bonfire," reveals Sansom's ability to sketch a self-righteous man, who entraps himself in a nightmarish bonfire, with vigor and irony. While many of his contemporaries raged against the British love of tradition, Sansom revered the past. As an acute observer of life around him and as a student of little masters such as Grandville and Bunin, Sansom knew how to make authentic a man or woman's sense of personal dignity. I believe his short stories will survive along with the best short stories of his time, with the short stories of Elizabeth Bowen, Graham Greene, Muriel Spark, Aldous Huxley, and William Golding.

Even though Sansom wrote many commercial or journalistic pieces, some of his novels and most of his short stories represent the best of his creativity and the best of traditional British literature. Perhaps his own words, among the last that he wrote, offer the best defense of his artistry. In writing an introduction to *The Gentleman from San Francisco and Other Stories* by Ivan Bunin, Sansom compares that author's short stories to "sonnets and odes, smaller jewelled architectures, the great little canvases of Brueghel—all 'little' masterpieces that soar far above so cosy an epithet as surely do the short works of Ivan Alexeyvitch Bunin, whose poetic and carefully economic prose has too often struck the unwary as 'sketchy.' To these one might whisper that Leonardo sketched pretty nicely, too."[15] These words apply to Sansom's short works as well.

Notes and References

Chapter One

1. "The Importance of Being Billy," Notebook, n. pag. This and other notebooks and typescripts are in the Berg Collection, New York Public Library.
2. "A Map of My Skin," Notebook, n. pag.
3. James Reeves, "Norman Cameron—Four Views," *Review* XXVII-XXVIII (Autumn-Winter 1971-72), 15-16.
4. Robert Graves, "Norman Cameron—Four Views," *Review*, p. 21.
5. "Coming to London," *Coming to London*, ed. John Lehmann (London, 1957), p. 135.
6. Ibid., p. 135.
7. Personal interview with William Sansom, 5 January 1975.
8. "Coming to London," p. 136.
9. Ibid., p. 137.
10. "Living in London," *London Magazine*, November 1970, p. 56.
11. Ibid., p. 57.
12. Frederick R. Karl, *Reader's Guide to the Contemporary English Novel* (New York, 1972), p. 7.
13. Personal interview with William Sansom, 5 January 1975.
14. "An Interview with William Sansom and Angus Wilson," *Queen*, March 1960, p. 143.
15. Ibid.

Chapter Two

1. As quoted in John B. Vickery's "William Sansom and Logical Empiricism," *Thought*, Summer 1961, p. 244.
2. Ibid.
3. "Fireman Flower," *Fireman Flower* (New York, 1944), p. 191.
4. Ibid., p. 194.
5. Ibid., p. 210.
6. Ibid., pp. 229-30.
7. Ronald Mason, "William Sansom," *Modern British Writing*, ed. Denys Val Baker (New York, 1947), p. 286.
8. "In the Maze," p. 111.
9. Ibid.

10. Erland Lagerroth, "Plot, Place and Idea in William Sansom's Writing," TS, pp. 18–19.

11. "In the Peach-House Potting Shed," *Fireman Flower*, p. 35.

12. Peter F. Neumeyer, "Franz Kafka and William Sansom," *Wisconsin Studies in Contemporary Literature*, VII, p. 82.

13. Paulette Michel-Michot, *William Sansom: A Critical Assessment*, (Paris, 1971), pp. 45–47.

14. Personal interview with William Sansom, 13 January 1975.

15. "The Long Sheet," *Fireman Flower*, p. 136.

16. Peter Nevile, rev. of *Fireman Flower*, *World Review*, July 1944, n.p.

17. Personal interview with William Sansom, 13 January 1975.

18. "The Cleaner's Story," *Three* (London, 1946), p. 15.

19. William A. Rossi, *The Sex Life of the Foot and Shoe* (New York, 1976), p. 249.

20. "The Cleaner's Story," p. 44.

21. "Grandville," *Pleasures Strange and Simple* (London, 1953) p. 80.

22. "The Cleaner's Story," pp. 49–50.

23. "The Equilibriad," *Among the Dahlias* (London, 1957), p. 183.

24. Ibid., p. 211.

25. Mason, "William Sansom," p. 290.

26. "The Vertical Ladder," *Something Terrible, Something Lovely* (London, 1948), p. 37.

27. "Something Terrible, Something Lovely," *The Stories of William Sansom* (Boston, 1963), p. 28.

28. Ibid., p. 33.

29. Ibid., p. 31.

30. Ibid., p. 36.

31. Ibid., p. 19.

32. Ibid., p. 27.

33. "Edgar Allan Poe," *Pleasures Strange and Simple*, pp. 82–86.

Chapter Three

1. Walter Allen, *The Modern Novel in Britain and the United States* (New York, 1964), p. 268.

2. *The Body* (London, 1949), p. 5.

3. Michel-Michot, *William Sansom*, p. 259.

4. John Woodburn, rev. of *The Body*, *Saturday Review* (27 August 1949), p. 11.

5. *The Body*, p. 65.

6. Ibid., p. 67.

7. Michel-Michot, *William Sansom*, p. 251.

8. *The Body*, p. 200.

9. Ibid., pp. 207–208.

10. Ibid., pp. 225–26.

11. Karl, *Reader's Guide to the Contemporary English Novel,* p. 284.
12. "The Compulsive Liar," *Man and Woman,* n.d., p. 743.
13. Ibid., p. 744.
14. Ibid., p. 744.
15. *The Face of Innocence* (London, 1951), pp. 233–34.
16. Ibid., p. 103.
17. Vickery, "Sansom and Logical Empiricism," p. 232.
18. *The Face of Innocence,* p. 102.
19. Ibid., p. 244.
20. Michel-Michot, *William Sansom,* p. 272.
21. Personal interview with William Sansom, 5 January 1975.
22. *A Bed of Roses* (London, 1954), p. 75.
23. Ibid., p. 105.
24. Ibid., p. 120.
25. Ibid., p. 206.
26. Michel-Michot, *William Sansom,* p. 292.
27. Personal interview with William Sansom, 13 January 1975.
28. "The Ulcerated Milkman," *The Ulcerated Milkman* (London, 1966).
29. *The Loving Eye* (London, 1956), p. 24.
30. Ibid., p. 110.
31. Ibid., p. 53.
32. Ibid., p. 71.
33. Ibid., p. 203.
34. Ibid., p. 202.
35. Letter received from Mario Praz, 15 December 1978.
36. *The Loving Eye,* p. 212.
37. Ibid., p. 245.
38. Ibid., p. 111.
39. Ibid., p. 133.
40. Ibid., pp. 23–24.
41. Ibid., p. 229.
42. Ibid., p. 55.
43. Ibid., p. 227–28.
44. Ibid., pp. 112–13.
45. Walter Havighurst, rev. of *The Loving Eye, Saturday Review* 40 (25 May 1957), 15.
46. David Daiches, *The Present Age in British Literature* (Bloomington, Ind., 1958), p. 321.
47. *The Cautious Heart* (London, 1958), p. 44.
48. Ibid., p. 57.
49. Ibid., pp. 143–44.
50. Ibid., p. 147.
51. Ibid., p. 156.
52. Ibid., p. 159.
53. Ibid., p. 170.

54. Ibid., pp. 175–76.
55. Ibid., pp. 75–76.
56. Ibid., pp. 40–41.
57. Mason, "William Sansom," p. 283.
58. *The Last Hours of Sandra Lee* (London, 1961), p. 39.
59. Ibid., p. 119.
60. Personal interview with William Sansom, 13 January 1975.
61. *The Last Hours of Sandra Lee*, p. 90.
62. Ibid., p. 136.
63. Ibid., pp. 189–90.
64. Ibid., p. 252.
65. Michel-Michot, *William Sansom*, p. 44.
66. Personal interview with William Sansom, 13 January 1975.
67. "Notes for Goodbye," Notebook.
68. Ibid.
69. *Goodbye* (London, 1966), p. 13.
70. Ibid., p. 21.
71. Ibid., p. 56.
72. Ibid., p. 101.
73. Ibid., p. 143.
74. Ibid., p. 90.
75. Ibid., p. 105.
76. Ibid., p. 153.
77. Ibid., pp. 216–17.
78. Anon., rev. of *Goodbye*, *New Statesman*, 21 October 1966, p. 72.
79. Anon., rev. of *Goodbye*, *Times Literary Supplement*, 27 October 1966, p. 973.
80. Personal interview with William Sansom, 5 January 1975.
81. William Foster, "Interview with William Sansom," *Scotsman*, 11 January 1975, n.p.
82. *Hans Feet in Love* (London, 1971), p. 221.
83. James Hughes, "Losing Hans Down in the Sex Stakes," *Evening Standard*, 14 September 1971, p. 20.
84. Personal interview with William Sansom, 5 January 1975.
85. Ibid.
86. *A Young Wife's Tale* (London, 1974), pp. 10–11.
87. Kay Dick, rev. of *A Young Wife's Tale*, *Scotsman*, 23 November 1974, n.p.
88. *A Young Wife's Tale*, p. 9.
89. Ibid., p. 144.
90. Ibid., p. 43.
91. Ibid., p. 58.
92. Ibid., p. 145.
93. Ibid., p. 223

94. Valentin Cunningham, "Provincial," *New Statesman*, 13 December 1974, n.p.

95. Anthony Thwaite, "Marital Frivolities," *Observer*, 17 November 1974, n.p.

Chapter Four

1. Personal interview with William Sansom, 13 January 1975.
2. "Tutti-Frutti," *South* (London, 1948), p. 79.
3. "Three Dogs of Siena," *South*, p. 102.
4. Ibid., p. 107.
5. Ibid., p. 120.
6. Kay Dick, "William Sansom," Brazilian Service of the B.B.C. "Letras Artes" 11 February 1954.
7. "A World of Glass," *The Stories of William Sansom*, p. 159.
8. Ibid., p. 167.
9. Ibid., p. 171.
10. "The Girl on the Bus," *The Stories of William Sansom*, p. 174.
11. Ibid., p. 177.
12. Ibid., p. 193.
13. "Episode at Gastein," *A Touch of the Sun* (London, 1952), p. 117.
14. Ibid., p. 118.
15. Ibid., p. 156.

Chapter Five

1. Elizabeth Bowen, introduction, *The Stories of William Sansom*, p. 8.
2. *Blue Skies, Brown Studies* (London, 1960), p. 13.
3. "A Contest of Ladies," *A Contest of Ladies* (London, 1956), p. 29.
4. Ibid., p. 44.
5. "The Last Word," *A Contest of Ladies*, p. 133.
6. "Various Temptations," *The Stories of William Sansom*, p. 68.
7. "Among the Dahlias," *Among the Dahlias* (London, 1957), pp. 15–16.
8. "Various Temptations," pp. 90–91.
9. "Among the Dahlias," p. 17.
10. "To the Rescue," *Among the Dahlias*, p. 47.
11. "The Man with the Moon in Him," *Among the Dahlias*, p. 179.
12. Ibid.
13. "The Waning Moon," *The Stories of William Sansom*, p. 195.
14. Ibid., p. 201.
15. "The Dangerous Age," *Among the Dahlias*, p. 80.
16. Ibid., p. 91.
17. Ibid., p. 96.
18. William York Tindall, *Forces in Modern British Literature, 1885–1946* (New York, 1947), p. 338.

19. "The Marmalade Bird," *The Marmalade Bird* (London, 1973), p. 92.

20. "Love at First Sight," *The Stories of William Sansom*, p. 88.

21. "The Ulcerated Milkman," p. 30.

22. Michel-Michot, *William Sansom*, p. 215.

23. "The Last Ride," *Among the Dahlias*, p. 147.

24. Ibid., p. 157.

25. Personal interview with William Sansom, 7 January 1975.

26. "A Visit to the Dentist," *Among the Dahlias*, p. 25.

27. Ibid., pp. 32–33.

28. "The Biter Bit," *The Marmalade Bird*, p. 156.

29. Chekhov as quoted in Ernest Simmons's *Chekhov* (Boston, 1962), p. 214.

30. "Down at the Hydro," *The Marmalade Bird*, p. 25.

31. "Mamma Mia," *The Marmalade Bird*, p. 72.

32. "A Day Out," *The Marmalade Bird*, p. 126.

33. "The Day the Lift . . . ," *The Marmalade Bird*, p. 53.

34. "Life, Death," *The Stories of William Sansom*, p. 286.

35. Michel-Michot, *William Sansom*, p. 218.

36. "Life, Death," p. 288.

37. Ibid., p. 292.

38. Personal interview with William Sansom, 13 January 1975.

39. "The Bonfire," *The Marmalade Bird*, p. 216.

40. Ibid., p. 218.

41. Ibid., pp. 219–20.

42. Ibid., p. 222.

43. Vickery, "William Sansom and Logical Empiricism," p. 193.

Chapter Six

1. "How the Story Was Written," *The Birth of a Story* (London, 1972), p. 45.

2. Ibid., p. 47.

3. Ibid., p. 53.

4. Ibid., p. 55.

5. John Brinner, rev. of *The Birth of a Story*, *Teacher*, 16 June 1972, n.p.

6. Anon., "One Man's Method," *Times Literary Supplement*, 16 June 1972, n.p.

7. *Proust and His World* (London, 1973), p. 106.

8. Peter Quenell, "The Professional's Proust," *Observer*, 30 September 1973, n.p.

9. Howard Nemerov, "Sansom's Fictions," *Kenyon Review*, Winter 1955, p. 130.

10. Introduction, *The Gentleman from San Francisco and Other Stories* (London, 1975), p. 7.

11. Vickery, p. 233.

12. Burgess, p. 109.

13. Malcolm Bradbury, ed., *Contemporary Writers on Modern Fiction* (Manchester, Eng., 1977), p. 10.

14. Evelyn Waugh, *The Ordeal of Gilbert Pinfold* (London, 1957), p. 1.

15. Introduction, *The Gentleman from San Francisco and Other Stories* (London, 1975), p. 7.

Selected Bibliography

PRIMARY SOURCES

Fireman Flower (1944). New York: Vanguard Press, 1945.
Three. London: Hogarth Press, 1946.
Westminster at War. London: Faber and Faber, 1947.
The Equilibriad. London: privately printed, 1947.
Something Terrible, Something Lovely. London: Hogarth Press, 1948.
South. London: Hodder and Stoughton, 1948.
The Body. London: Hogarth Press, 1949.
The Passionate North. London: Hogarth Press, 1950.
The Face of Innocence. London: Hogarth Press, 1951.
A Touch of the Sun. London: Hogarth Press, 1952.
It Was Really Charlie's Castle. London: Hogarth Press, 1953.
The Light That Went Out. London: Hogarth Press, 1953.
Pleasures Strange and Simple. London: Hogarth Press, 1953.
Lord Love Us. London: Hogarth Press, 1954.
A Bed of Roses. London: Hogarth Press, 1954.
The Loving Eye. London: Hogarth Press, 1956.
A Contest of Ladies. London: Hogarth Press, 1956.
Among the Dahlias. London: Hogarth Press, 1957.
"Coming to London," *Coming to London.* Ed. John Lehmann. London: Phoenix House, 1957, pp. 128–42.
The Cautious Heart. London: Hogarth Press, 1958.
The Icicle and the Sun. London: Hogarth Press, 1958.
Blue Skies, Brown Studies. London: Hogarth Press, 1960.
The Last Hours of Sandra Lee. London: Hogarth Press, 1963.
The Stories of William Sansom. London: Hogarth Press, 1963.
Get-Well Quick Colouring Book. London: André Deutsch, 1963.
Illus. for *Who's Zoo*, by Michael Brande. London: André Deutsch, 1963.
Away to It All. London: Hogarth Press, 1964.
The Ulcerated Milkman. London: Hogarth Press, 1966.
Goodbye. London: Hogarth Press, 1966.
The Grand Tour. London: Hogarth Press, 1968.
Christmas. London: Weidenfeld and Nicolson, 1968.
The Vertical Ladder. London: Chatto and Windus, 1969.
"Living in London," *London Magazine* 10: 8 (Nov. 1970), 52–64.
Hans Feet in Love. London: Hogarth Press, 1971.
The Birth of a Story. London: Hogarth Press, 1972.
"The Compulsive Liar," *Man and Woman* 2: 27 (n.d.), 743–45.

The Marmalade Bird. London: Hogarth Press, 1973.
Proust and His World. London: Thames and Hudson, 1973.
Victorian Life in Photographs, ed. London: Thames and Hudson, 1974.
A Young Wife's Tale. London: Hogarth Press, 1974.
Skimpy. London: Hogarth Press, 1974.
"The Impossibility of Being Billy," TS. William Sansom papers. Berg Collection, New York Public Library.
"A Map of My Skin," TS. William Sansom Papers. Berg Collection, New York Public Library.
SANSOM, WILLIAM. Personal interviews. 5, 7, 13 January 1975.

SECONDARY SOURCES

The criticism of Sansom's work is limited almost wholly to transitory reviews of the novels and collections of short stories; therefore, only a few scholarly and critical articles devoted to him are listed in the secondary sources.

ALLEN, WALTER. *The Modern Novel in Britain and the United States*. New York: E. P. Dutton, 1964. Discusses why Sansom appears to be a maverick compared with his peers.
BOWEN, ELIZABETH. "Introduction," *The Short Stories of William Sansom*. Boston: Little, Brown and Co., 1963. pp. 7–12. A gracious introduction to Sansom's art of conveying hallucination, scenery, and the senses by one of his principal exponents.
BURGESS, ANTHONY. *The Novel Now*. New York: W. W. Norton, 1967. Observes that writers such as Rex Warner and William Sansom, who began as Kafka disciples, do not continue in writing about nightmare for long. Calls *The Body* a superb book and appreciates Sansom's lyricism in it and in subsequent novels.
DAICHES, DAVID. *The Present Age in British Literature*. Bloomington: Indiana University Press, 1958. Contains brief commentary on Sansom's early work.
GINDIN, JAMES. *Postwar British Fiction: New Accents and Attitudes*. Berkeley and Los Angeles: University of California Press, 1962. Gives a good analysis of themes and fads of Sansom's contemporaries.
KARL, FREDERICK. *Reader's Guide to the Contemporary English Novel*. New York: Octagon, 1972. A good appraisal of Sansom's potential for being a first-rank novelist. Says Sansom needs to expand his range by choosing less trivial themes and shallow characters. Appreciates his comic talent. Makes a case for comparison of Sansom with Henry Green in superficial ways because both write on a small scale but finds that Green makes his world seem large while Sansom does not.
MASON, RONALD. "William Sansom," *Modern British Writing*, ed. Denys Val Baker. New York: Vanguard, 1947, pp. 281–91. A thoughtful

analysis of Sansom's realism and symbolism in early works. Mason hypothesizes about Sansom's potential to develop from a nightmare miniaturist into a powerful and imaginative artist.

MICHEL-MICHOT, PAULETTE. *William Sansom: A Critical Assessment.* Paris: Société d'Edition "Les Belles Lettres," 1971. Originally written as a doctoral dissertation at the University of Liège, this is a very valuable book for careful explications of all his work published up to 1966. Concludes that his short stories are first rate while his novels are not.

NEMEROV, HOWARD. "Sansom's Fictions," *Kenyon Review,* Winter 1955, pp. 130–35. An analysis of Sansom's strengths in observing scenes and people with insight and weaknesses in overelaborate prose and descriptions that do not support or reflect the central fable of each work.

NEUMEYER, PETER F. "Franz Kafka and William Sansom," *Wisconsin Studies in Contemporary Literature* VII (Winter-Spring 1966), 76–84. A contrast and comparison of illusion and reality as presented in Kafka's works and Sansom's early short stories.

RABINOWITZ, RUBIN. *The Reaction against Experiment in the English Novel 1950–1960.* New York: Columbia University Press, 1967. Useful in placing Sansom along with Henry Green as writers more concerned with style and form and less with themes than their peers.

TINDALL, WILLIAM YORK. *Forces in Modern British Literature, 1885–1946.* New York: Knopf, 1947. An interesting study of experimental and traditional fiction.

VICKERY, JOHN B. "William Sansom and Logical Empiricism," *Thought* 36: 141 (Summer 1961), 231–45. A philosophical essay on the surrealist effects achieved by Sansom in his early fiction.

WEST, PAUL. *The Modern Novel.* London: Hutchinson, 1963. Groups Sansom with Anthony Burgess, Rex Warner, P. H. Newby, Gabriel Fielding, and Rayner Heppenstall as writers who deal with "the poetic, the subjective and the metaphysical" as opposed to the writers of "class-picaresque."

Index

153